O TASTE
AND
SEE

O TASTE AND SEE

A BIBLICAL REFLECTION
on EXPERIENCING GOD

BONNIE THURSTON

PARACLETE PRESS
BREWSTER, MASSACHUSETTS

2014 First Printing

O Taste and See: A Biblical Reflection on Experiencing God

Copyright © 2014 by Bonnie Thurston

ISBN: 978-1-61261-407-6

Library of Congress Cataloging-in-Publication Data.
Thurston, Bonnie Bowman.
  O taste and see : a biblical reflection on experiencing God / Bonnie Thurston.
    pages cm
  Includes bibliographical references.
  ISBN 978-1-61261-407-6 (pb french flaps)
  1. Spirituality—Christianity. 2. Experience (Religion) I. Title.
  BV4501.3.T518 2013
  248.2—dc23   2013026069

10 9 8 7 6 5 4 3 2 1

Published by Paraclete Press
Brewster, Massachusetts
www.paracletepress.com
Printed in the United States of America

FOR THE SISTERS OF DIVINE PROVIDENCE

Marie de la Roche Province:

in thanksgiving for

making God's providence visible

and for our shared experiences thereof.

CONTENTS

¹ I will bless the LORD at all times;
   his praise shall continually be in my mouth.
² My soul makes its boast in the LORD;
   let the humble hear and be glad.
³ O magnify the LORD with me,
   and let us exalt his name together.

⁴ I sought the LORD, and he answered me,
   and delivered me from all my fears.
⁵ Look to him, and be radiant;
   so your faces shall never be ashamed.
⁶ This poor soul cried, and was heard by the LORD,
   and was saved from every trouble.
⁷ The angel of the LORD encamps
   around those who fear him, and delivers them.
⁸ O taste and see that the LORD is good;
   happy are those who take refuge in him.
⁹ O fear the LORD, you his holy ones,
   for those who fear him have no want.
¹⁰ The young lions suffer want and hunger,
   but those who seek the LORD lack no good thing.

¹¹ Come, O children, listen to me;
 I will teach you the fear of the LORD.
¹² Which of you desires life,
 and covets many days to enjoy good?
¹³ Keep your tongue from evil,
 and your lips from speaking deceit.
¹⁴ Depart from evil, and do good;
 seek peace, and pursue it.

¹⁵ The eyes of the LORD are on the righteous,
 and his ears are open to their cry.
¹⁶ The face of the LORD is against evildoers,
 to cut off the remembrance of them from the
 earth.
¹⁷ When the righteous cry for help, the LORD
 hears,
 and rescues them from all their troubles.
¹⁸ The LORD is near to the brokenhearted,
 and saves the crushed in spirit.

¹⁹ Many are the afflictions of the righteous,
 but the LORD rescues them from them all.
²⁰ He keeps all their bones;
 not one of them will be broken.
²¹ Evil brings death to the wicked,

and those who hate the righteous will be
condemned.
22 The LORD redeems the life of his servants;
none of those who take refuge in him will be
condemned.

Some bits of Scripture are for an individual forever associated with a place and a time, and thereby become part of the furniture of the heart. Psalm 34:8a is such a phrase for me: "O taste and see that the LORD is good," or in the form deep rooted in my heart, "O taste and see how gracious the Lord is."

In the mid-1970s I was a graduate student at the University of Virginia and fully subject to the influences of those heady days. I was also led by Providence to St. Paul's Memorial Episcopal Church, which became one of the formative influences in my life. It was a lively and progressive place, full of the sort of people I wanted to be "when I grew up." The parish's "crown" was wonderful liturgy and an extraordinary music program directed by one of the professors of music at The University. I sang in the choir for five years and learned a great deal about musicianship, the range of English church music, and most importantly, dedication, friendship, and loving God with the body, in that case, the voice.

It was there, in what was then the rather dank choir room in the church basement, that I first heard (and sang) R. Vaughn Williams's glorious setting of "O taste and see." It was one of the composer's last sacred pieces, written for the coronation of Queen Elizabeth II (and thus is only a tiny bit younger than I am). One treble voice slices through the silence, and then, in vaguely pentatonic mode, other voice parts take up in a deceptively simple-sounding, canon-like structure the psalmist's extraordinary invitation to "taste God" and "see God." Wait a minute! Isn't God incorporeal? Spirit (John 4:24)? Doesn't *God* say, "You cannot see my face; for no one shall see me and live" (Exod. 33:20)? And yet here are twin imperatives to perceive God's Providence *viscerally*, in our bodies.

When I read Psalm 34, as I do monthly in making my way through the Psalter at the Daily Offices, when I come to 34:8 I always hear Vaughn Williams.[1] It was his music and St. Paul's choir that first led me to ponder this verse, to taste its ideas, eat them, ruminate on them (to use a visceral metaphor). This tiny phrase, buried as it is in the Psalter, is one of the great keys of Judeo-Christian-Islamic spirituality and one of the church's lost missionary invitations.

I believe, and I hope this little book will demonstrate, that it contains monotheistic theology in a nutshell, perhaps the shell of Dame Julian of Norwich's hazelnut with its focus on God's love and grace. But when there is a hunger for God (a hunger built into the structure of the human person), it is not so much for theology as for the *experience* of God. The great human hunger is not first for theology (although, ironically, this little book opens with theology). Theology comes after satisfying the primary hunger, which is for direct experience of God. We *do* believe in order to understand. We first want to *know* God, not "about" God. When God has been experienced, then language (theology) can, but not necessarily must, be made about the experience.

Psalm 34:8 contains in miniature the whole process of coming to and growing in faith. It gives us insight into God and into how we experience God. Oddly enough (but perhaps not since our God has, in creation and history, demonstrated a certain sense of humor), this is most clear when one looks at the constituent parts of Psalm 34:8 *backwards*, when one meditates on the last bits first. I don't think this is what Jesus had in mind when he (repeatedly) declared the last would be first, but it certainly works as an approach to this snippet of psalm.

The last two phrases of the half verse tell us two fundamental things about God: first, *that* God is ("the Lord is"); and second, *how* God is ("gracious" or "good"). Everything else we know about God flows from those two assertions. The first two phrases suggest how we can experience God. It seems to me that the church has traditionally conducted evangelism and education with the assumption that God is best experienced first by the mind or understanding. Christian education and catechesis typically invites us to "see" God by means of the intellect. We get "lessons" of one kind or another. Of course, sight is the great and pervasive scriptural metaphor for understanding. But in light of my own experience, I wonder if we church people don't need to explore more fully the fact of experiencing God more viscerally, in the body. A particular example of this, for me, is precisely the phrase "O taste and see," which I first began to understand by means of the body, by singing it. Certainly in Christian tradition, which grows from the soil of the mystery of the Incarnation, of God incarnate in the person of Jesus, both *body* and knowing by means of the body deserve more attention than they have been given. (Parenthetically, I suspect we aren't taught this way because our church leaders weren't. As a former seminary professor, I saw precious little by way of the experiential in seminary. Seminaries were preparing students for further graduate school, not necessarily for the parishes into which some 90 percent of them were planning to go. Little wonder half of new clergy leave the ministry in the first seven years.)

In any case, Psalm 34:8 gives insight into the fact *that* God is and *how* God is, and suggests that we can experience God by mind/knowing/understanding ("see") and by our viscera and our senses ("taste"). Together the sum is greater than the parts; the invitation is to a delight in God and God's self-communication, which feeds a hunger basic to human beings in every era of history and in every culture. But most parish churches are only feeding their parishioners at "subsistence level." (Pastors can't take us where they themselves have not been.)

If you think you might be hungry for God, but haven't experienced God directly, or if you are a believer who still feels malnourished, I hope this little book might be for you a kind of manna. Taste. See. If you are fed, thank God who is gracious and who has always provided and is always providing heavenly food.

PART
ONE

1

THE PHRASE
Text and Context

Most of this book muses on the experience of God using the phrase from Psalm 34:8, "Taste and see that the LORD is good," as a template. But, as I hope anyone who has studied Scripture with me would attest, it's dangerous to take a biblical phrase out of context. As Margaret M. Daly-Denton has so succinctly noted, "Context always contributes to comprehension."[2] So we begin our exploration with a brief, and I hope not too technical, discussion of the Psalter itself, where Psalm 34 occurs in it, and what type of psalm it is. We'll look at the phrase within the structure of the psalm, provide some notes on its translation, and close with a few comments on its use in the church, keeping in mind that the Psalms are a rich repository of experiences of God (and sometimes of God's absence).

This is the most "academic" bit in the book, and you may choose to skip it.

One reason I love the Psalms is that you don't have to get dressed up to pray them. When I was a child, you had to get dressed up, put on your best clothes to go to church. Somehow this morphed into the idea that I had to get psychically "dressed up" to pray, had to put my best self and *only* my best self before God. Who did I think I was kidding? In the Psalms there is no dress-up, no costume. It's "just as I am," naked emotion and not all of it pretty.

In introducing an edition of the Psalms in the King James Version Kathleen Norris writes, "The Psalms are blessedly untidy."[3] Even the worst human emotions are brought into the open and put before God.[4] In an essay written in the 1950s, Cistercian monk Thomas Merton suggests that we are ". . . not to learn from the Psalms a totally new experience, but rather to recognize, in the Psalms, our own experience lived out and perfected, orientated to God and made fruitful." Merton says, "There is no aspect of the interior life, no kind of religious experience, no spiritual need . . . that is not depicted and lived out in the Psalms."[5]

Nothing human is foreign to the Psalms. They accept us as we are in our "undressed-up" state. Indeed, they suggest that fancy dress gets in the way of prayer. Because human emotion is expressed so directly, is so "unvarnished" in the Psalms, they invite us to an honesty in our own prayer that is crucial. God doesn't require "fancy dress." Who we are and what we are "wearing" from moment to moment is what God longs for. "Cleaning up our act" in prayer is not being totally honest, and it is total honesty that fosters communication with God.

The voice of the psalmist invites me to be honest with God. Conversely, the English Benedictine Sebastian Moore remarks that "God behaves in the psalms in ways he is not allowed to behave in systematic theology."[6] If we are allowed to be who we are in the Psalms, so is God. The God of the Psalms is as various as the voices we meet in them. The Psalms remind us we are dealing with a God who has said unequivocally, "My ways are not thy ways" (see Isa. 55:8–9).

Another reason I love the Psalms is that they unite me with the ancient tradition of both Israel and the church. The Psalms represent a communal tradition of prayer, even when I pray them alone. They save me from the tyranny of individual- ism. William L. Holladay subtitles his wonderful book on the history of the Psalms in the church "the prayerbook of a cloud of witnesses."[7] This reminds me that in praying a psalm, I am enter- ing an ancient tradition. "Used as private prayer, the Psalms unite us to the praying church," says Thomas Merton, "because the Psalms are always the church's prayer."[8]

THE PSALTER IN THE HEBREW BIBLE

But the Psalter predates Christianity. The book of Psalms is first of all a book of Hebrew Scripture and song. Before Jesus, the Psalms existed as Israel's expression of relatedness to God. As the Carmelite and scholar Fr. Roland Murphy (of blessed memory) points out, the writers of the Psalms "were not aware of the existence of a future life with God. For them life in the here and now included a relationship with God, and they appreciated this relationship deeply." Murphy continues, "Faith has . . . to do with God and a full-hearted acceptance of God."[9]

The Psalter occurs in the section of the Hebrew Bible known as the "Writings," where it appears as *Tehillium*, "hymns" or "songs of praise." When Hebrew Scripture was translated into Greek, the word *psalmoi*, or "songs," was used. (The Greek translation is called the Septuagint.) The canonical Psalms are the final stage of a process that took several centuries. Although some go back to the time of King David and before, the Psalms as we have them were probably collected by the Temple personnel of the Second, or postexilic Temple. (The return from exile was ca. 380 BC.) It's difficult to date the Psalms, although in some there are clear indications of a pre- and postexile divide, which provide within individual psalms themselves indications of when they were written. Some, for example, are "of David" (3, 7, 18, 34, 51, 52, 54, 46–47, 59, 60, 63, 142) or give a time reference (for example "destroyed your temple," or "by the waters of Babylon"). All of the psalms reflect a long heritage, come from many stages in Israel's history, and represent Israel's fundamental reality as a worshiping community. We see reflected in them the covenant at Sinai, the central sanctuary at the time of Joshua, the United Kingdoms of David and Solomon, laments over the exile, and joy of return and rebuilt Temple.

Before we turn to the structure of the book of Psalms, a quick clarification is in order. The numbering of psalms and verses within psalms differs in different translations. There is nothing very difficult (and certainly nothing nefarious) about this. The numbering system followed by most Protestant translations uses that in the Hebrew text. Roman Catholic translations tend to follow the numbering in the Septuagint and subsequent Latin (Vulgate) translations. There are exceptions, such as the New American Bible–Revised Edition, which follows the Hebrew numbering. Either way, the difference is in the numbering, not the content of the Psalms.

Within the book of Psalms, then, scholars have delineated five "collections" on the basis of repeated doxologies. A Talmudic Midrash (explanation) on Psalm 1 explains that as Moses gave five books of law to Israel, so David gave five books of Psalms. The oldest attestation of this fivefold division is a liturgical fragment from a Qumran document (1Q30) dating to the turn of the first century AD. The following is a rough outline of the five "books" with some notes about their contents:

Psalm 1: Introduction to the book

Book 1: Psalms 2–41

   (41:13 doxological conclusion)

   While these psalms vary in content, they are united by use of Yahweh (YHWH, the Tetragrammaton, or "four letters") for the Divine Name and *le dvd*, or "by-David," psalms. Fifty-six of the seventy-three "by-David" psalms appear in the first two books of Psalms. *Le* can mean "by" or "to" or "concerning" and thus can indicate either authorship by or honoring of or information about David.

Book 2: Psalms 42–72

   (72:18–19 doxological conclusion)

   These psalms use "Elohim" for the Divine Name. Many scholars think they are from the period of the monarchy.

Book 3: Psalms 73–89
(89:52 doxological conclusion)
Book 3 contains mainly "Elohistic psalms,"
and many have "Asaph" as superscription.

Book 4: Psalms 90–106
(106:48 doxological conclusion)
Psalms 93–100 seem to be a traditional
collection of throne-accession hymns,
that is, psalms that were sung upon the
enthronement of a new king.

Book 5: Psalms 107–149
This section contains 120–34, the
"Songs of Ascent," a pilgrimage collection, with one psalm for each step up to
the temple.

Psalm 150: Doxology for the whole book.[10]

PSALM 34 AND OUR THEME VERSE 34:8

Psalm 34, in which our theme phrase appears,
occurs in book 1 of the Psalter and is a psalm *le
dvd*, "of David." The full historical superscription,
which was probably added by a later scribe, is
a little confused. It says, "Of David, when he
feigned madness before Abimelech, so that he

drove him out, and he went away." "Abimelech" seems to be in error if the reference is to the story in 1 Samuel 21:10–15, in which the ruler is Achish. Mitchell Dahood's general description is more helpful: "A psalm of thanksgiving composed by an individual whose prayer for deliverance from tribulations was heard by Yahweh."[11]

Dahood's comment reminds us that scholarship examines the Psalms according to forms with particular patterns. The most common form in the Psalter is the lament (isn't *that* interesting?), followed by the "hymn" or praise form. Roland Murphy describes Psalm 34 as "a thanksgiving psalm with wisdom influences."[12] Such psalms are closely related to the hymn form and follow the general structure of a cry to extol or praise followed by a story of deliverance. They "tend to draw a lesson from the experience and to proclaim publicly the Lord's faithfulness."[13] (Please note the emphasis on experience, a matter with which this book concerns itself.) Comments in the New Interpreter's Study Bible divide the first half of Psalm 34 according to Murphy's pattern. Verses 1–10 are a testimony of thanksgiving, focusing in verses 4–10 on an experience of being delivered.[14] Most scholars note that verses 11–22, with their use of admonitions and proverbial sayings, are in the mode of wisdom teaching.[15] What is not evident in English translations is that Psalm 34 is an acrostic in Hebrew (like Psalms 25, 37, 111, 112, 119, 145). Verses begin with the letters of the Hebrew alphabet, although for some reason the Hebrew letter *vav* is omitted and a summary verse is added at the end.

Within verses 1–10 I find four "movements" on the part of the psalmist. Verses 1–3 are a general expression of praise and thanksgiving that invite the reader/singer to participate (v. 3). Verses 4–7 describe the specific reason/event that evoked the thanksgiving: God delivered. Verse 4 is the "hinge" of the section, asserting that the psalmist sought and that God answered and delivered. (The Grail edition of the Psalter movingly points out that 34:5 is the verse St. John Fisher recited when he saw the sun shining behind the scaffold upon which he was to die.[16]) Verses 8–9 then command the reader/singer to experience God and respond appropriately. Note that the first half of the Psalm describes intense activity on the part of the speaker: blessing and praising (v. 1), boasting (v. 2), magnifying (v. 3), seeking (v. 4), looking (v. 5), crying (v. 6), tasting and seeing (v. 8), as well as calling for activity on the part of the hearer: fearing (which means "holding in awe," v. 9) and seeking (v. 10). Verse 10 serves as a summary of the first half of the psalm, which continues in verses 11–22 with a wisdom teaching about *how* to "fear the LORD." In the first half of the psalm, the psalmist suggests that spiritual experience is not passive, nor should one accept by hearsay the existence and activity of God. The invitation is to personal experience. Verse 8 is part of the speaker's exhortation, his "double imperative invitation to perceive God's provision."[17]

I found it enlightening to compare the major English translations of 34:8a. The most common translation is "Taste and see that the LORD is good." The most interesting variations were Eugene Peterson's paraphrase in The Message, "Open your mouth and taste, open your eyes and see—how good God is,"[18] and Mitchell Dahood's rendering in his Anchor Bible commentary, "Taste and drink deeply, / for Yahweh is sweet."[19] Dahood explains that "taste" comes from the Hebrew *ta'mu*, meaning "savor" and "drink deeply." It is "semantically cognate with *rawah*," meaning "to be saturated, drink one's fill." Dahood believes "Yahweh is sweet" is correctly translated by the Vulgate's *quoniam suavis est Dominus.*[20]

Because the writers of the New Testament wrote in Greek, which became the primary language of the primitive church, I did a little exploration of my own in the Greek lexical field of Psalm 34:8, *geusasthe kai idete hoti chrestos* in the Septuagint. *Geusasthe* comes from the same verbs at the root of the English words "gustation" and "gustatory." *Geuo* means "cause to taste," and *geuomai* means "to taste, to eat, to have perception of, to experience." It is so used in Hebrews 6:4–5, which speaks of having "tasted the heavenly gift" and "tasted the goodness of the word of God and the powers to come." First Peter 2:3 paraphrases our verse: "You have tasted that the Lord is good." Apparently the earliest "Christians," who were Jews steeped in the Psalter, understood "taste" to be a metaphor for coming to know something intimately.

There are several verbs for "to see" in Greek. The Septuagint chooses *idete*, a form of *horao*,

which was in fact rare in popular, common language. Its dictionary definition is "to see, observe,
notice, perceive, understand." ("To see" is the great
Johannine metaphor for "to understand." We'll
return to this point in chapter 4.) Interestingly *The
Vocabulary of the Greek New Testament* notes that this
form is used in the Septuagint "for appearances
of the Divinity and similarly by Paul."[21] This is
corroborated by W. F. Arndt and F. W. Gingrich's
famous Greek lexicon, which finds instances of the
form used "of the perception of personal beings
that become visible in a supernatural manner" and
"of beings that make their appearance in a supernatural manner."[22] To see is to perceive with the
eye, but *horao* implies that it is also to understand
what one perceives, perhaps especially of divinity.

The commands (for they are imperatives) to
"taste and see" are calls to experience and to
understand what is experienced about the Lord
(*ho kyrios*). The psalmist calls us to taste and see
that the Lord *is*, and therefore acts in a particular
way. The Lord is "good." The adjective *chrestos*
can translate a whole range of virtues: "kind,
loving, good, merciful." In secular literature the
term was used to mean "virtuous" or "excellent,"

that is, morally good, of excellent character. For classical philosophers "good" meant conforming to the moral order of the universe. In Scripture the term characterizes the Creator of the universe. St. Luke uses this word to describe God, who "is *kind* to the ungrateful and the wicked" (6:35). The early church made much of the fact that "good" (*chrestos*) sounds like "Christ" (*Christos*), and I shall provide a wonderful example of this below. In the meantime, I note that the etymology of these Greek words suggests that if we are to know what is essential about a being (i.e., one who exists), we must first experience it with our senses (taste, sight), secondarily recognizing that the senses can be metaphors for understanding.

The Psalter and Psalm 34:8
in the Church

We noted above that the Psalter was "borrowed" (perhaps "appropriated" is a better term) from Judaism by the early Jesus believers. The Psalter was first a book of Hebrew Scripture, so it is not surprising that the early Jesus believers, most of whom *were* Jews, mined it to help them understand their Lord. The church used the Psalms as a way to understand Jesus (especially Psalm 110) and Jesus's experience (especially Psalm 22). Roland Murphy explains that the New Testament's "appropriation was along two main lines. First, the messianic interpretation of the royal psalms (e.g., Pss 2 and 72). . . . Second, . . . many psalms of lament were viewed as having a bearing on Jesus's suffering and death (e.g., Pss 22 and 69)."[23] Just as the Psalter was the "hymn book of the second Temple," it became the heart of the church's liturgy, especially the Daily Offices in monastic liturgy. Both John Cassian and St. Benedict devote chapters in their rules to how, how many, and when the Psalms are to be used in the Daily Office.

Our phrase, Psalm 34:8, became associated with the most sacred aspect of Christian worship, the Eucharist. St. Augustine (d. 430) reports that a psalm was sung by a cantor during the distribution of Communion in Carthage. St. Cyril of Jerusalem (d. 386) reports that for that event "the prescribed psalm portion is Psalm 34:9 (8)."[24] William Holladay notes, "During the liturgy of the faithful, at the distribution of the communion bread, Ps. 34:9 (8) is sung. . . . because of a shift of pronunciation in Greek, a wonderful word play has emerged. . . . *crestos* (good) is now heard as *Christos*—'Taste and see that *Christ* is the Lord.'[25] According to the Orthodox Study Bible, "Verse 8 is seen throughout the Orthodox Church as describing the act of receiving the Body and Blood of Christ"; thus Psalm 34 is a favorite Orthodox psalm at reception of Communion.[26]

It was perhaps from the association of Psalm 34:8 with Holy Communion that one of the most charming folk uses of the verse arose. No religion exists only in its purest form; all have entered into the imagination of believers, from whence many—sometimes spurious—folk practices arise. One such folk belief taught that the verse "could be used to prevent wine from turning; one was instructed to write the verse on an apple and then throw the apple into the wine."[27] (After a day or so I'd like to "taste and see" how the apple fared!)

The importance of the Psalms in Christian tradition is evident in their continued presence in liturgy and hymnody. A few examples will suffice to make the point. Gregorian chant, of course, arose as a particular musical form in which the Psalter could be sung in the monastic choir. While much was jettisoned at the Reformation, the tradition of psalm singing was preserved by German Lutherans in particular and by the Scots tradition of metrical psalm singing, which itself influenced the hymnody, especially shape-note singing, in the American South. Modern hymnbooks still contain many metrical psalms. For example, Psalm 34 ("New Version," 1696) appears in hymnals as "Through All the Changing Seasons," and is often sung to the tune Wiltshire C. M. (George T. Smart, d. 1867).[28] Following Benedictine practice in the development of its offices, the Anglican/Episcopal Church preserves the chanting of psalms, especially at Morning and Evening Prayer and Compline.

We can enter into the experience of the Psalter from many levels and points of view. There is the level of history, which we have briefly explored here by looking at the Psalter's Jewish origin, its structure, and the form and vocabulary of an individual psalm (Ps. 34), as well as its adaptation by Christians. Psalms are poems, and as such are multivalent. Any given psalm has multiple levels of meaning and is best approached through the situation of the speaker, the form chosen, and metaphors used. Most importantly, psalms are prayers that we are invited to pray ourselves and to apply to our own lives.[29] The remainder of this book is an extended meditation, a kind of *lectio divina* on steroids, on the phrase "Taste and see that the Lord is good."

As the introduction indicated, we'll be considering the phrase "backwards." This is not scholarly perversity on my part, but a logical progression beginning with God's "is-ness" or existence (the Lord *is*) and then the manner of that existence (good) and how we come to know it: by seeing (a metaphor for understanding, rational knowledge) and by tasting (a metaphor for existential knowledge).

Looking at the phrase in its context in the Psalter has suggested that we keep in mind the communal context of the psalms. Although they address personal experience, they were collected for communal worship. Meditating on psalms can be a profound point of connection with two religious traditions and their adherents. Psalm 34:1–10 has a particular focus on the *activity* of seeking God. Its speaker seeks and cries, is answered and delivered, and so invites the hearer to "magnify the LORD with me" (v. 3), to "look to him and be radiant" (v. 5), to "taste and see" (v. 8), to "fear the LORD" (v. 9). When people seek God, God responds. That should draw forth a response from people. The seeking described in Psalm 34:1–10 is active and visceral. It takes a mouth to bless, boast, magnify, cry, and taste. It takes eyes (of the head and of the heart) to seek, look, see. It takes ears to hear. The "soul makes its boast in the LORD" (34:2) because the body and the heart have sought and been found by God. At the most basic level this means that God *is*. The search that Psalm 34 describes presumes the existence of the One sought. It is to God's existence that we now turn.

2

THE LORD *IS*

Fools say in their hearts, 'There is no God'"(Ps. 14:1 and 53:1). Thus the psalmist twice tidily disposes of the question of the existence of God. The writers of the Hebrew Bible (and the world of the ancient Near East in general) assumed the existence of God. The combination of violent horrors and scientific insights of the last two centuries has made the matter far more complex for contemporary people. So, frankly, have we Christians who, largely through thoughtless familiarity, have nearly completely domesticated the wildly improbable and outrageous claims of our faith.[30]

Since in modern Western culture we can no longer assume God's existence, we begin our meditations on Psalm 34:8 with its last phrase, "the LORD is." We consider *that* God is in this chapter, and then *how* God is in the next.

Philosophically speaking we are thinking about God's existence and manifestations. I begin by admitting that I can't "prove" God's existence and that, in any case, "belief" or "faith" isn't the same thing as "certainty." Faith has more to do with hope and trust than with certainty. Br. David Steindl-Rast, OSB, suggests that "faith is profound trust in the actuality to which beliefs point."[31] There is a subtle distinction between "belief," which may be based on evidence of some sort, and "faith," which is a matter of trust and hope.

With this distinction in mind, Alister McGrath's book *"I Believe": Exploring the Apostles' Creed* helpfully reminds us that "I believe in God" is only one way of translating the creed's original Latin opening phrase, *Credo in Deum*. He suggests more accurate translations would be "I trust in God" or "I am of the opinion that there is a God." Faith, he notes, "cannot be equated with knowledge. It is not a cold and cerebral idea, enlightening the mind while leaving the heart untouched. Faith is the response of our whole person to the person of God."[32] For McGrath "'I believe in God' means 'I have committed myself to God.' To believe in God is to belong to God."[33]

No one can commit someone else to something. In his book on the Apostles' Creed, Br. David Steindl-Rast comes to a similar conclusion. He reminds us that in Latin *"Credo* is a compound of *cor* ('heart') and *do* ('I give') and means literally 'I give my heart.'"[34] In other words, *credo* means that "I dedicate myself in complete trust to a power greater than myself."[35] In the glossary at the back of his classic work *Gratefulness, The Heart of Prayer*, Br. David includes the following in his definition of faith: "To have faith does not primarily mean believing something, but rather believing in someone. Faith is trust. It takes courage to trust."[36]

What I am suggesting by quoting these very different writers is that "belief" in God involves commitment that is personal and volitional, and that encompasses the whole person, not just intellectual assent. In this it is a great deal like love. Catherine de Hueck Doherty is correct: "Faith is a country of darkness into which we venture because we love and believe in the Beloved, who is beyond all reasoning, all understanding, all comprehension."[37] Perhaps I lead us into a "country of darkness" when I invite us to consider "the Lord *is*."

This chapter, which begins our "backward journey" through Psalm 34:8, does not attempt to prove God's existence. One reason it doesn't is, frankly, that I am neither an apologist nor a systematic theologian and so don't have the "tools" for "proofs." What I do here is, first, to share two reasons why I, personally, believe in God; second, to suggest two ways in which biblical writers speak of God's existence, or "is-ness"; and, third, to offer the suggestion that the sentence "God is love" (1 Jn. 4:8) gets it right in the proverbial nutshell.

Honestly, I am (almost!) mute before the mystery of my own faith. I don't know why I have it. *That* I have it I know is a grace, a gift, something given and received, not "figured out" or earned, something for which I am profoundly grateful. I believe God *wants* to give the gift of faith and that those who surrender and ask, receive it, but in God's way and God's time. For me belief involves a huge experiential component. Logically, one can't experience what doesn't exist, and I have *experienced* what I take to be God in the natural world and in the faith of other people.

I was born and grew up in one of the remotest and wildest areas of the United States, the coalfields of the southern Appalachians, where Virginia, West Virginia, and Kentucky come together. My dad was a mining engineer, and I lived my early life in coal camps up "hollers" and at the end of mountain roads, places of breathtaking beauty and ruggedness. I played within sight of what I was told was one of the last stands of virgin timber in the East. As far back as I can remember, I experienced "presences," or perhaps a "Presence," in the natural world. Nothing in nature seemed inanimate.

When as a high school student I read Gerard Manley Hopkins's sonnet "God's Grandeur," I recognized its truth in my very cells.

The world is charged with the grandeur of God.
  It will flame out, like shining from shook foil;
  It gathers to a greatness, like the ooze of oil
Crushed. Why do men then now not reck his
  rod?
Generations have trod, have trod, have trod;
  And all is seared with trade; bleared,
    smeared with toil;

And wears man's smudge and shares man's
    smell: the soil
Is bare now, nor can foot feel, being shod.

And for all this, nature is never spent;
    There lives the dearest freshness deep
    down things;
And though the last lights off the black West
    went
    Oh, morning, at the brown brink eastward,
    springs—
Because the Holy Ghost over the bent
    World broods with warm breast and with
    ah! bright wings.[38]

In spite of the human-made smear and blear and smudge, the natural world and its processes have always been for me an inexhaustible source of knowledge about and experience of God. This is because I believe God created it all and resonate deeply with poet Denise Levertov's "amazement at the existence of anything at all when God could have rested in his own all sufficiency."[39] She observes in her poem "Primary Wonder," "the quiet mystery / is present to me."

that there is anything, anything at all,
let alone cosmos, joy, memory, everything,
rather than void: and that, O Lord,
Creator, Hallowed One, You still,
hour by hour sustain it.[40]

In her engaging book *Theology for Skeptics: Reflections on God*, German theologian Dorothee Soelle says, "This ontological surplus of Being in the face of Nothingness is what the Christian religion . . . tries to articulate."[41]

Indeed, God's immanence, God's presence in what God created, is a first point in St. Paul's Letter to the Romans. He argues that the wicked are "without excuse; for though they knew God, they did not honor him as God or give thanks to him" (Rom. 1:20–21). They knew God because God is evident in what God made. "For what can be known about God is plain to them, because God has shown it to them. Ever since the creation of the world his eternal power and divine nature, invisible though they are, have been *understood and seen through the things he has made*" (Rom. 1:19–20, italics mine). In short, God makes God's self known in creation. This has been my experience.

It has also been my experience that God makes God's self known through believers. I was blessed by my "human geography" as well as by the physical place I grew up. I was surrounded by mountains and by believers. I shared the circumstance of the psalmist: "I have been entrusted to [God] ever since I was born; / you were my God when I was still in my mother's womb" (Ps. 22:10, BCP). My maternal grandfather was a pastor; his wife and daughter (my grandmother and mother) sang to me and taught me about Jesus. I was taken to church, no easy thing for my father, who drove our old, green Dodge over the winding, pocked roads to town on Sunday. Church and school (where most of our teachers were unabashedly Christian) were the loci of life. My friends were, for the most part, churchgoers.

As I grew (in stature—and girth—if not in wisdom!), I had the wit to stay around church people. I went to our church's college when ties between church and college were still strong and a form of *in loco parentis* was still operative. I was led to a wonderful parish in graduate school that, while it didn't save me from the sins and errors of young adulthood, didn't abandon me to them either. I married a pastor and into his (varied: Pentecostal, Evangelical, and Orthodox!) Christian family. As an adult I observe the difference faith makes to people as they face the challenges of life, the "slings and arrows . . . flesh is heir to." In recent years it's been my privilege to work and associate with communities of religious men and women and with monastics. Their faith and wisdom humbles and sustains me.

All of this (embarrassing) personal revelation simply corroborates the point the writer makes in chapters 11 and 12 of the Letter to the Hebrews. That writer's famous definition of faith, "the assurance of things hoped for, the conviction of things not seen" (11:1), is followed by a long list of examples of the biblical faithful and the startling conclusion that "they would not, apart from us, be made perfect" (11:40). Chapter 12 opens, "We are surrounded by so great a cloud of witnesses. . . . " And for me the great, unbroken chain of faithful historical witnesses is a "proof" of God's existence. If there is no God, a lot of impressive and very intelligent people over several thousand years have been badly deluded. Logically that seems to me unlikely.

The Bible is many things, but one of them is an ancient witness *that* people believed in God and recorded something of the nature of their belief. Fundamental to their understanding was that God is personal and, as such, has a name. In the entry "GOD (Biblical and Christian)" in *The Encyclopedia of Religion and Ethics*, W. T. Davison writes that the existence of God was presupposed by Old Testament writers. From the outset the idea of God was simple and concrete, not meta-physical and not abstract. What would they have made of the phrase from the liturgy of St. John Chrysostom: "For you are the ineffable God, inconceivable, invisible, incomprehensible"? For them, God was personal.[42] Personality implied "a living Being . . . who possessed all the character-istics of a personal life . . . a distinctive feature of the God of the Old Testament throughout."[43] They believed that "the Lord *is*," that God is personal, not an inchoate or amorphous process behind the manifest universe.

God is "person," but not exactly person as we experience individuals. For example, the writer of Genesis asserts, "God created humankind in his image, in the image of God he created them;

male and female he created them" (Gen. 1:27). This means that God is in some way *both* male and female, that without the feminine *and* masculine we do not have the perfection of God. In his startlingly titled book *God: A Biography* (which caused a great stir when it was published in 1995), Jack Miles writes that God is ". . . an amalgam of several personalities in one character."[44] God is male *and* female; Father, Son, *and* Spirit, personal but different from persons as we experience them. I introduce this point because a common image of God as Über-Male is a stumbling block to belief for some people. In a reflection on Exodus 3:14 John F. Kavanaugh writes, "There is no other way to talk about who and what God is other than to say that God is existence itself. Am-ness. God is the holy ground of being. At the bottom of the universe is not some mindless grinding machinery or evolutionary process. What moves everything, from stars to human hearts, is personal existence."[45]

YHWH is the personal name of the God of Israel. There is an extraordinary story in Exodus 3 in which Moses asks God, in effect, "What is your name?" (3:13). The matter of a name (*shem*) was no small thing in the biblical world. "Name" was understood to be part of the soul, representing its essence, not an arbitrary label to honor a deceased family member (or rock star). Thus to speak "in the name" of someone was to share in his or her authority (as the great eighth-century prophets of Israel shared in God's). If you knew someone's name, you really *knew* them and could, in fact, manipulate them on the basis of that knowledge. For Moses to ask God's name is an act of considerable effrontery and cheekiness. It is surprising that God answered at all. But then, God is *personal*, and how could people call upon an "unnamed" Person?

God's prehistoric, personal name is revealed as YHWH, a name attested 6,600 times in Hebrew Scripture and by the ninth-century BC Moabite Stone.[46] The word "LORD," spelled with capital letters, the Tetragrammaton (four letters), stands for the Divine Name, which is too holy and powerful to be spoken. It derives from the Hebrew verb *hayah*, "to be," and is variously translated "I AM WHO I AM" or "I AM WHAT I AM" or "I WILL BE WHAT I WILL BE." Studies of the meaning of this enigmatic name abound.

Three interpretations have dominated scholarly discussion. The Septuagint translation (from Hebrew to Greek), *Ego eimi ho on*, is "I am the one who is," emphasizing God's eternal being and divine will. The first-century Jewish philosopher Philo and the medieval Jewish philosopher Maimonides and most of the church fathers assume this reading. (We hear it echoed in the *Ego eimi*, "I Am," sayings of Jesus in John's Gospel.) The Masoretes (rabbinical scholars of ca. AD 700) emphasized the causative form of "to be," thus interpreting the name to mean "the one who causes to be," the Creator. The name could also be translated by the simple future tense, "I will be," which makes God's name a promise of presence, a promise that God is turned toward God's people and will be with them. This is what the text of Exodus 3:7–12 suggests: "I have observed the misery of my people"; "I know their sufferings, and I have come down to deliver them"; "The cry of the Israelites has come to me; I have seen . . ."; and "I will be with you."

I owe a great deal of my understanding of The Name to my former (beloved and revered) colleague Donald Gowan, particularly to his extraordinary book *Theology in Exodus*, which devotes four very rich chapters to Exodus 3–4. Gowan points out that YHWH "had no definition, as the names of other gods did (*Baal* means 'master'; *Anu* means 'sky,' etc.)."[47] The enigma of The Name was intentional. It preserved God's "otherness." It was so mysterious that a second "name-giving" account appears in Exodus 6:2–8, in which "the new thing signified . . . is that God now means to fulfill the promises of Genesis."[48] The point is God's involvement in human history, God's involvement in change. "Yahweh is not a definition, but a designation; he is 'the One who is intervening here.'"[49] Gowan summarizes, ". . . the invisible God—who is pure spirit, whom we can never truly comprehend, and who can certainly never adequately be denoted by some words in human speech—that God becomes a person to us, whom we can address and whom we feel we know to some extent, when he gives us a name by which we can call him."[50]

What strikes me about the "name giving" in Exodus 3 is that the name given is not, as we might expect, a proper *noun* or even an adjectival form (like my own first name), but a *verb*, an indication of action. God is not thing, but being, Being itself (as per Kavanaugh above). God is, indeed, *actively* with us and *in* the processes of history and creation. The controversial feminist theologian Mary Daly suggested this many years ago, writing, "Why indeed must 'God' be a noun? Why not a verb—the most active and dynamic of all? . . . isn't the Verb infinitely more personal than a mere static noun? The anthropomorphic symbols for God may be intended to convey personality, but they fail to convey that God is Be-ing."[51] God, Daly suggests, is "the Verb of Verbs."[52] This is not, Dorothee Soelle explains, a matter of parts of speech but of new ways of thinking about transcendence as bound up in the web of life.[53] And this is critical, because Soelle thinks that God is "irrelevant" for the great majority because of God's "non-interference."[54] Nouns are static. Verbs interfere.

The verb "to be" is the verb of existence, and in the personal realm, "existences" come into being through love. If this is true in the human sexual realm (and that, apparently, is God's plan), then it must to some degree be true in the spiritual realm because human beings, like God Who Is

Being, are unified, one being. Many of us learned as children that "God is love," and it takes a lifetime to glimpse what 1 John asserts: "Love is from God; everyone who loves is born of God" and "God is love" (see 1 Jn. 4:7–21). In his 1976 Bampton Lectures, G. W. H. Lampe said, ". . . the primary mode of the presence of God's Spirit . . . is chiefly mediated through human love." And "We experience the presence of God in our relations with other human beings."[55] In fact, on every level, we love each other into being. Hugh of St. Victor wrote that God dwells in the human heart in two ways, through knowledge and through love; ". . . yet the dwelling is one, since everyone who knows Him loves, and no one can love without knowing."[56]

Discovering God in experience can, but need not be, dramatic. It may have to do with paying attention to the data of our own ordinary and everyday circumstances and experiences, to look here and not elsewhere for God. That would entail struggling against a distractedness that is now endemic and almost everywhere manifested by a general inability to turn off the electronic gadgetry and pay attention to what is right here in the present moment rather than somewhere off in the ether. It also would entail a return to life in the body, to the senses and the extraordinary data they wonderfully communicate to us every moment.

Coming to the *is*-ness of God may be a gradual coming to awareness that involves accepting what God wants to give. Like love, "knowing God" involves the vulnerability of surrender, the perhaps whimpered admission "I need." In John 4 Jesus himself initiated relationship by means of his need for a drink of water. The inability to exhibit such "divine vulnerability" is one reason why it is so difficult for many people to experience genuine intimacy in relationship and, perhaps, belief and faith in God.

Belief and faith can begin with even a tentatively whispered, "I need," which bespeaks the humility to accept what God wants to give. And this is why expressing need it is so difficult for so many of us. Knowing God means accepting both personal insufficiency and another's help. Put another way, faith is a matter of accepting a gift. "That God IS" comes with a promise of presence and the gift we call "grace." It is the subject of the following chapter.

3

THE LORD IS *GOOD*

Having thought a bit in the last chapter about Psalm 34:8's assertion of the *fact* of God, God's existence, or Is-ness, we now turn to the matter of *how* God is. It would, of course, be impossible to describe all God's qualities or characteristics.[57] They are beyond human perception and understanding. But Psalm 34 illustrates a number of God's characteristics, primarily those of deliverer (34:5–7, 17, 19), hearer of prayer (34:15, 17), comforter (34:18), and redeemer (34:22). Another of the psalmist's descriptions of God is that " the LORD is merciful and gracious, / slow to anger and abounding in steadfast love" (103:8; compare 145:8–9).

A bit of theological history might help us with our inquiry (if it doesn't put us to sleep!). In the fourth century, Basil of Caesarea, one of that extraordinary trio of Cappadocian fathers, distinguished between the essence or substance of God and God's "divine energies." God was understood to be one essence in three personal modes (*mia ousia en trisin hypostasesin*), each of whom has its own characteristic properties. Basil's insight is that God is essentially constituent (God is God) and also has divine attributes (properties or characteristics that emanate from the divine nature). Humans can't know God's essence, but we can experience God's characteristics.

This accounts for the basically analogical (comparative) depiction of God in Hebrew Scripture and in much Christian discussion of God. For example, God is *like* (has the characteristics of) a king or a judge or a shepherd. "For the Israelite, God's deeds reveal not that He is but what He is."[58] When we closed chapter 2 with an allusion to the fact that love constitutes God's fundamental relationship to creation (one of the great insights of St. Thomas Aquinas, d. 1274), we had begun to consider God's "energies," or "how God is." The psalmist's great invitation in 34:8 is to "taste and see that the LORD is *good*." It is God's characteristic "goodness" or "graciousness" to which we now turn, beginning by revisiting a bit of word study.

Because it sounds like "Christ," you'll probably remember that the word for "good" in the Septuagint (Greek) version of Psalm 34:8 is *chrestos*, which has a range of meaning, including kind, loving, good, and merciful. In secular Greek the word basically meant excellent, useful, good of its kind. "When used of people the term means 'worthy,' 'decent,' 'honest,' morally 'upright' or 'good.'"[59] The Septuagint uses the word as an attribute of God and God's goodness and mercy. Even God's severity in punishing transgressors of the law presumes God's goodness because God's ordinances *must* be good because God *is* perfect goodness. This is the premise of the long meditation on the law that is Psalm 119.[60]

In the New Testament, Luke's Jesus says that the Most High "is kind [*chrestos*] to the ungrateful and the wicked" (Lk. 6:35). Another important use of the term is found in Romans 2:4 in which

Paul has *to chreston* as a noun to describe the divine kindness which allows space for repentance, but which the impenitent disdain and hence store up wrath for themselves. What is meant is God's gracious restraint in the face of . . . people's sins prior to Christ. *chrestotes* . . . occurs again in 11:22 with reference to God's gracious act in Christ. As Paul sees it, kindness constantly characterizes God, but this kindness finds particular expression and completion in his saving work in and through Christ.[61]

This related term, *chrestotes*, is used by the Apostolic Fathers in relation to God's "saving work in Christ and more generally to his fatherly acts as Creator, Sustainer, Redeemer and Consummator."[62] All this etymology points to what Christian tradition calls God's graciousness. What we are considering in thinking about God's goodness is one of Christianity's central theological concepts, grace.

In contradistinction to popular images of God the great judge and punisher of sinners (an image dear to several of the regular cartoonists in *The New Yorker* magazine), God the hurler of thunderbolts (sounds to me more like Zeus or Thor), God the recorder of misdemeanors in heaven's Big

Black Book, Psalm 34:8 invites us to experience the goodness, the grace of God. I suspect modern people may be more concerned with God's apparent silence or absence than with God's goodness, but that is another discussion for another time (perhaps for an extended meditation on Psalm 22:1–2 or Psalm 88).

I have never quite understood the prevalent fixation on the juridical God. It seems contrary to the contents of the Bible. At most there are four books of law in Hebrew Scripture. The books of the Bible are primarily narratives that depict God taking the initiative to be in relationship with and to care for human beings. Why is it easier to remember the prophet Joel's words of judgment than his great promise in 2:13 that "the LORD, your God . . . / is gracious and merciful, / slow to anger, and abounding in steadfast love, / and relents from punishing"?

The paradigmatic image of this occurs in Genesis 3, after Eve and Adam have snacked on the forbidden fruit. God strolls through the Garden of Eden in the cool of the evening seeking to be *with* the humans, who ". . . hid themselves from the presence of the LORD God among the trees of the garden" (Gen. 3:8). God seeks to be with us; we hide from God, perhaps because at some level we *know* we've messed up. As the Genesis story continues, God punishes human disobedience but does not "curse" Adam and Eve as God does the serpent in 3:14. God also "made garments of skins for the man and for his wife, and clothed them" (Gen. 3:21). God's judgment is tempered with mercy and practical care for the man and woman.

In Jewish tradition, law is God's great gift to human beings. Mostly on the basis of awkward or inaccurate readings of St. Paul, we Christians often don't "get" this. God wants human beings to be in relationship with God and with each other and, via the law, gives the parameters in which this can most fruitfully and happily occur. (That foundational story, interspersed with the law itself, is told in Exodus, Leviticus, and Numbers.) But, like Adam and Eve, the biblical Hebrews have trouble obeying the law. God does not give up on them, although early on it's touch and go in Genesis 6 and 7. After generations of enduring our human tendency to "hide among the trees," God sends the prophets to call people back to Divine Goodness.

For example, in Ezekiel 24 the prophet delivers God's condemnation against the "shepherds of Israel," who look after themselves rather than their sheep, and God's promise to be Israel's shepherd. Via Ezekiel God promises: "I myself will search for my sheep, and will seek them out." God promises to rescue them, gather them, feed them, to seek the lost, bring back the strayed, bind up the injured, and strengthen the weak (see Ezek. 34:11–16; then compare Jer. 23:1–4). Of course the best gloss on this passage is Psalm 23: "The LORD is my Shepherd, I shall not want." In Luke 15:3–7 Jesus uses the shepherd metaphor in a parable, and in John 10:1–18 Jesus describes himself as the "good shepherd."

Admittedly, when Jesus speaks of God, he does not omit the image of God as judge. The Matthean Jesus is particularly interested in God's judgment. But the Lukan Jesus focuses on God's *chrestos*, which can, of course, be manifested in judgment, because good and loving parents must sometimes punish recalcitrant and disobedient children. God's *chrestos* is perhaps most vividly depicted in the well-known and beloved parable in Luke 15 of the prodigal son, his equally unsavory older brother, and their extraordinarily gracious father. In the parable, the sons repeatedly insult the father. The younger asks for his inheritance *before* the father dies, an inexcusable affront. "So he divided his property between them" (15:12). The older son refuses to share the joy of his brother's return; he won't even call him "brother" (Lk. 15:30: "this son of yours"). The older son has made the host leave his party, a terrible insult. Amazingly, just as the father was on the road watching for the younger son's return, so also the father comes out to beg the older son to come to the party because "all that is mine is yours" (15:31).

"How gracious the LORD is!" To quote Psalm 103 again, "As a father has compassion for his children, / so the LORD has compassion" (103:13). God is not the cosmic kid who takes names while the teacher is out of the room. Nor is God the cosmic accountant putting red hash marks in the negative column under my name in the Book of Big Sins. (And, believe me, God could legitimately do that!) God is the Creator who wants to walk with, to visit with his creatures in the cool of the evening, the loving parent who has already given the child more than his due, watched him leave, and then stood looking up the road waiting to welcome him home with a party. God is the great initiator of relationship with humans *in spite of* their (my) wandering from, misunderstanding, and actively insulting God.

The New Testament provides ample evidence of the assertion in Psalm 34:8 that God is good, that God is gracious. St. Paul is perhaps the most famous biblical articulator of this concept, which he may have learned in the great schools of Tarsus, or in Gamaliel's school in Jerusalem, but which he experienced on the road to Damascus. He *thought* he was helping God out by persecuting "heretical" Jesus Jews. But, on the Damascus Road, Paul learned he was quite mistaken. He was doing something really wrong, but God had *already* "fixed it." As he wrote to the church at Rome, "God proves his love for us in that while we still were sinners Christ died for us" (Rom. 5:8). In describing his dramatic reorientation Paul says "God . . . called me through his *grace*" (Gal. 1:15, italics mine). Philippians 3:1–4:1 is Paul's extraordinarily personal revelation of what this call from God meant. In this passage, Paul makes clear that what has become important to him is not his family tree, the accomplishments on his resume, or his ego strength, but that "Christ Jesus has made me his own" (Phil. 3:12).

Paul understands God's graciousness primarily "in God's saving work for sinners (Romans 5:8)."[63] As J. I. Packer pointed out some years ago in his book *Knowing God*, Paul's understanding of God's graciousness involves a whole series of presuppositions "the spirit of our age is . . . directly opposed to."[64] These presuppositions include the idea of ourselves as creatures fallen from God's image, that God is not true to the divine nature (goodness) if sin goes unpunished, and that "To mend our relationship with God . . . is beyond the power of any one of us."[65] The good news is God's grace offered *in spite of* human demerit. "It is God showing goodness to persons who deserve only severity."[66] The New Testament does not tell the story of human depravity but of "how our Judge has become our Saviour."[67] The good news proclaimed by Paul, and by other New Testament writers, is that "in Christ God was reconciling the world to himself, *not counting their trespasses against them*" (2 Cor. 5:19, italics mine).

At the root of this wonderfully shocking idea that we *don't* get what we deserve is that Christ "takes the rap" for us. The theological word for this is atonement: defined as "'at-one-ment' . . . the end-effect of the process of redemption: being at one with God (from whom we were previously alienated) and so sharing in the divine life."[68] Atonement is one of those theological ideas on which much ink has been expended over a very long period of time. It occurs in Judaism and finds its focus in Yom Kippur, the annual Day of Atonement (see, for example, Leviticus 16). In Christianity its center is the crucifixion of Jesus.

During Lent one year, I was facilitating a quiet day, and a participant told me about her three-year-old grandson who was absorbed by, nearly obsessed with, the crucifixion. He was interested in crucifixes and depictions of Jesus's death in art. He had so many questions about Jesus's death that his grandmother wondered if it were normal. I said I thought it was unusual, but not abnormal. Children who have been loved and nurtured can respond with great sensitivity to the sufferings of others, especially to random suffering and the suffering of innocent people. I can relate to that little boy's concern. Questions abound. *Why* (the quintessential two- and three-year-old question) punish a good person? *Why* did Jesus have to suffer and die? *How* did the crucifixion erase sin? *What kind of God is this?* It is outrageous to assert that God died on a Roman cross, Rome's horrific instrument of "deterrence" saved for non-Roman citizens, insurrectionists, and the most terrible criminals.

Much better minds and much better Christians than I have addressed these and related questions. What I say comes only from my observation of human experience, and you may not like it. In a broken relationship, only the wronged party can restore the relationship because only the wronged party can forgive. I know that state-ment *seems* to put the onus on the victim, but in fact it shifts the balance of power *to* the wounded person. The wounder can ask for forgiveness. But only the wounded can give it, and so only the wounded can effect reconciliation and restore relationship. To make the theological analogy: Christians see God's goodness in God's extraordinary response to humans, who broke relationship with God, whether through eating forbidden fruit, breaking given commandments, or just wandering away in callous indifference to God and God's creation. God offers reconciliation by becoming one of us and dying. I know it's unlikely, but there it is.

For many, if not most, contemporary people, the great *skandalon*, the stumbling block, to believing God's goodness and accepting God's graciousness is the idea that we can't do it for ourselves. America in particular lives by the great cultural myth of the rugged individual who is completely self-sufficient. Of course this has never been true, as attested by the clustered huts of Pilgrims who would have starved had they not been assisted by the original Americans, and by the snaking wagon trains headed westward. In the global economy of our day, neither individuals nor nation states are self-sufficient. But the issue here is personal: admission of need manifested by a deep and volitional decision to accept from God what I can't do for myself. Some folks turn up their noses at the Billy Graham crusades, but his old hymn of invitation, "Just as I am, without one plea," is spot on. Recognizing this is the first step. Surrendering to God is the second.

Surrender is another word that elicits negative responses. A local private school has as its motto "Never, never, never give up." But sometimes, especially in the psycho-spiritual life, giving up or surrendering is the bravest, truest, strongest, and best course of action. The moment I raise a tentative white flag in God's direction, God responds, as the father did to his rather priggish and nasty older son in the parable, "you are always with me, and all that is mine is yours" (Lk. 15:31).

Herein lies another indication of the goodness of God. God has entrusted all that is God's to us: all creation, what the Book of Common Prayer calls "the vast expanse of inter-stellar space." Everything, and especially the well-beloved only Son, is given to us. What Gerard Manley Hopkins's sonnet "Spring" wonderfully calls "all this juice and all this joy" is freely offered to us.[69] As we noted in considering the existence of God in Psalm 34:8, God reaches out to us through what God created. But we don't always accept what is offered.

In his wonderful book *Things Seen and Unseen: A Catholic Theologian's Notebook*, Lawrence Cunningham recalls an interview that the writer Saul Bellow gave to *Le Monde*. "While speaking about the secularization of France, he said that nobody in France believes in God, and thus God ends up sitting in a café all day long. God, in France, is not hidden; God is emeritus."[70] Having recovered somewhat from the shock of the idea that human beings have the power to "pension God off," to retire God from active service while allowing God to retain some vestige of impotent divine rank, I see the accuracy of the observation. God effectively becomes "emeritus" when we lose touch with gratitude for all that we have been given, first of all for the miracle of life itself, which none of us did anything to deserve or create.

God's goodness is evident in life-giving generosity of all sorts. I have tried to express God's yearning goodness in the following poem, titled "Iris."

> Iris are the exhibitionists
> of early summer gardens,
> true to etymology,
> rainbows of pink, purple, puce.

Color of the eye,
Iris was Juno's messenger,
carried her dispatches
from heaven to earth,
so often used the rainbow
to pass between them
that Jupiter's jealous queen
by metamorphosis
made her a rainbow.

Isaiah understood that
before sealing promises,
thus our own God
created this motley universe,
thereby pleading, "Here I am,
Here I am. Love me."

God is. And God is manifested in the world by "energies," characteristics, qualities like goodness and graciousness. God's goodness is primarily manifested by the verb love. God is love. And to know love, you have to surrender to it. All the beautiful thoughts about love, all the important philosophical musings, can't begin to touch the powerful and humanizing experience of being *totally* knocked-off-your-donkey *smitten* by it, as having had this extraordinary experience, I can attest.

We *know* love by surrendering to it. I was deeply moved when someone who comes to me for spiritual companioning described her surrender to God's love and her response to it as getting down on her knees "just to love God back." We know God by surrendering to God's goodness manifested to us in a continual reaching out in love. The verse "O taste and see how good the LORD is" invites us to this experience, and surrender is the crucial, affirmative RSVP. What it might mean to "see" God's goodness is the subject of the next chapter.

PART
TWO

4

EXPERIENCING GOD
Seeing

The following fragment of a Sioux prayer provides a wonderful transition to the second half of this meditation on Psalm 34:8:

. . . Great Spirit, you have been always, and before you nothing has been. There is no one to pray to but you. The star nations all over the heavens are yours, and yours are the grasses of the earth. You are older than all need, older than all pain and prayer. . . . Great Spirit, fill us with the light. Give us the strength to understand and the eyes to see.[71]

Like the psalmist and the writer of Genesis, the Sioux who prayed this prayer believe "in the beginning . . . God" (Gen. 1:1), that God created

the heavens and the earth, and that God grants
the ability to "see," to understand. Such seeing
requires a certain strength that only God can give.

The First Peoples who prayed this prayer knew
that it is God who grants the gift of this sort of
sight, a fundamental understanding of Christian
theology as well. In his highly accessible book
on the creed, Karl Barth notes almost at the outset, "Only God's revelation, not our reason . . .
can carry us over from God's incomprehensibil-
ity." Barth continues, "It is not because we have
already sought Him that we find Him in faith but,
it is because He has first of all found us that we
seek Him. . . ."[72] The capacity to know God—for
sight is a metaphor for understanding (a point to
which I shall soon return)—is the result of God's
initiative. As I have been suggesting, God always
makes the first move. Humans may or may not
respond to the invitation.

Thus far we have pondered God's existence
and the manner of it. We now turn to what I
hope is the heart of this extended meditation on
Psalm 34:8: the matter of *how* we might "know"
God. The psalmist suggests that we can "see"
and "taste." We'll consider seeing as a biblical

metaphor for understanding in this chapter and "tasting," giving the body to, in the next, and in the conclusion I will link these two "ways" or "paths" to the Word and Sacrament of worship in Christian tradition.

Wouldn't you expect it by now? We begin with etymology. There are several words for "see" in Greek, each with its own subtle connotation. Two common "see verbs" are *blepo* and *horao*. On the one hand, forms of *blepo* usually refer to physical sight, "with a stronger emphasis on the function of the eye."[73] On the other hand, forms of *horao* can suggest either physical sight or understanding. In Hellenistic religious writing, the Septuagint, and the first-century Jewish philosopher Philo, *horao*'s "main use is for spiritual perception."[74] As noted in chapter 1, the imperative form of *horao* appears in Psalm 34:8, which I might paraphrase "Hey! You! *See* [that is, "understand" via experience] how good God is!"

While I certainly don't deny that there is an important intellectual component to faith (I did spend nearly thirty years as a university and seminary professor), I don't think it's what the psalmist had in (um) mind. *Pace* the

Enlightenment philosophers, I'm not sure that "rationalism" or "intellectual proof" is the predominant mode for experiencing God. Jacques Maritain opens his lovely study *Approaches to God* with the admission that God "IS inaccessible yet . . . close at hand" and that "there are as many ways of approach to God as there are wanderings on the earth or paths to [man's] own heart."[75] He discusses "prephilosophic knowledge of God," "philosophical knowledge of God" (via St. Thomas Aquinas), and "ways of the practical intellect." Interestingly, he closes his study, not with a conclusion, but with questions: ". . . how could the intellect, knowing God in His effects, fail to aspire to know Him in Himself? It is natural and normal that, knowing a reality . . . from without and by means of signs, we should desire to know it in itself and to grasp it without intermediary."[76] In short, with regard to God, the great desire of the human heart is to "taste and see," to experience directly and *bodily*.

But doesn't the Bible say that we can't see God and live? Yes indeed, and with practical consequences for our inquiry. When he intercedes for the people after they have made the golden calf,

Moses (who has the chutzpah to ask outrageous questions and make astonishing requests) brazenly asks God, "Show me your glory, I pray" (Exod. 33:18). To which God replies, "I will be gracious . . . and will show mercy. . . . But . . . you cannot see my face; for no one shall see me and live" (Exod. 33:19–20). God apparently grants an exception for Moses at this crucial phase of Israel's wilderness sojourn. Thereafter, apparently, no one physically sees God and lives, I suspect for three reasons. First, God is too bright and splendid and glorious and beautiful and holy. We could not bear it. It would vaporize us. Second, as noted, God is *person*; God is not material. We can't see God the way we see objects because God isn't a thing. Jesus explains this to Nicodemus in John 3 and in John 4 tells the Samaritan woman theologian, "God is spirit" (John 4:24). Third, this accounts for the distinction we made in chapter 3 between God's essence and God's manifestations, God's being and God's energies. We see God in what God has created. To see that God is good is to "see through" created things to Who stands behind them. "All these creatures," says the Upanishad, "have their root in Being."[77]

Especially beauty in all its forms can provide easy access to God. For example, Islam teaches that God was a hidden treasure desiring to be known, so God created the world in order to be known. Thus the Prophet reasons in a Hadith that traces or sparks of divine beauty awaken love for God. In a reflection on Gerard Manley Hopkins's phrase "juice and joy," Bishop Robert F. Morneau pens a spin on Edna St. Vincent Millay's "I am waylaid by beauty." He writes, "Beauty is out to get us and lies in ambush to surprise us at every turn. This phenomenon is a holy, graced attack awakening us to the marvels and splendor of creation."[78] Nearly all religious traditions and many of our great poets have highlighted the connection between beauty and the experience of God.

Since God, for a variety of reasons, can't be seen in the *blepo* way, the biblical writers often use the verb "see" (*horao*) to mean "understand," which is why the writer of Ephesians prays that the eyes of their hearts might be enlightened (Eph. 1:18). The end of the book of Job and St. John's Gospel provide powerful examples of this sort of heart seeing.

Job is a disturbing book. It opens with a prose narrative that scholars suggest is an immensely old folktale about an innocent man who loses everything (including his children) but not his faith. He responds like the prophet Habakkuk, who says,

> Though the fig tree does not blossom,
> and no fruit is on the vines;
> though the produce of the olive fails,
> and the fields yield no food;
> though the flock is cut off from the fold,
> and there is no herd in the stalls,
> yet will I rejoice in the LORD;
> I will exult in the God of my salvation.
> (Hab. 3:17–18)

Job closes with another bit of narrative, which doesn't, for me at least, quite compensate for what God has allowed to happen to him and to his unpleasant wife (Job 1:6–12; 2:1–8). The poetic middle of the book (chapters 3–31) is composed of three cycles of dialogue in which Job's friends Eliphaz, Bildad, and Zophar assure him that he must have sinned, or God wouldn't

be punishing him. (With friends like these . . .)
To which Job replies (in effect), "I didn't; I didn't;
I didn't," and continues to plead the case of his
innocence before God.[79] Then, losing patience
with the "old guys" ('twas ever thus), a young
man, Elihu, breaks in to lecture Job about the
educative value of suffering (chapters 33–35) and
to issue a challenge to look for God's purposes in
everything (chapters 36–37, especially 37:14).
Elihu isn't interested in the assumed connection
between sin and suffering. He wants to turn Job's
eyes outward toward God's majesty and work in
nature.

In my reading, Elihu helps Job move from a
focus on his own, unarguably tragic, circumstances to the fate of humans in general. Elihu
says, in effect, "look around you, Job." At this
point (chapter 38), God enters the discussion
and, depending upon how one reads the book,
either affirms Elihu's point of view or changes the
subject. I'd like to hear the tone of the divine
Voice in 38:4 as God asks Job, "Where were you
when I laid the foundation of the earth? / Tell
me, if you have understanding." There follows
in chapters 38 and 39 an extraordinary and

energetic catalog of God's work in creation. God doesn't answer Job's questions or vindicate his innocence. God invites Job to recall God's majestic creation. Job gets the point, "See, I am of small account; what shall I answer you? / I lay my hand on my mouth" (40:4), whereupon God continues descriptions of his (more esoteric: the Behemoth, the Leviathan) creatures.

The crux comes in 42:1–6, with Job's realization that he has spoken out of turn. He realizes the error of the *way* he has spoken ("I have uttered what I did not understand, / things too wonderful for me, which I did not know," 42:3), though not necessarily the error of the question he has asked. The crucial verse is 42:5: "I had heard of you by the hearing of the ear, / but *now my eye sees you*" (italics mine). Sitting there in the dust, covered with sores, Job has heard a lot of secondhand theology (from his pals), but *now* he has had direct, personal experience of God. A note in *The New Oxford Annotated Bible* explains, "God has not justified Job, but he has come to him personally; the upholder of the universe cares . . . so deeply that he offers him the fullness of his communion. Job is not vindicated but he has obtained far more than a recognition of innocence; he has been accepted by the ever-present, master-worker, and intimacy with the Creator makes vindication superfluous."[80] Job has been brought into the near presence of God and *sees*. He moves from theoretical knowledge about God to an experience *of* the living, engaged (if perhaps still inscrutable) God.[81] Job "sees" God and lives.

Turning to John's Gospel, almost anyone who has read almost anything about the Fourth Gospel knows that "seeing" is one of the Evangelist's primary theological metaphors. John's prologue (1:1–18) opens, "In the beginning," and offers a new explanation of the creation story (1:1–5, 10–13) which culminates "And the Word became flesh and lived among us, and *we have seen* his glory" (1:14, italics mine). John the Evangelist establishes his authority on the basis of what has been seen, directly experienced.[82] Not surprisingly, then, the First Letter of John opens by explaining that what follows is an account of what was experienced: "what we have heard, what we have seen with our eyes, what we have looked at and touched with our hands" (1:1); "we have seen . . . and testify" (1:2); "we declare to you what we have seen and heard" (1:3). Yes, these are all forms of *horao*.

Jesus first appears in John's Gospel when John the Baptist "sees" (form of *blepo*) him and says, "I myself have seen [form of *horao*] and have testified that this is the Son of God" (1:34). John understands what his eyes have perceived. In the next scene, John's disciples watch (form of *blepo*) Jesus walk by, and John says, "Look [form of *horao*], here is the Lamb of God!" (1:35–36). They ask Jesus, "where are you staying?" and he replies, "come and see" (1:39, form of *horao*). This invitation is one way that John the Evangelist makes the connection between personified divine Wisdom in the Old Testament and Jesus.

Wisdom in both Hebrew (*hokmah*) and Greek (*sophia*) is feminine in form, thus the biblical figure of Lady Wisdom, who appears in Job 28; Proverbs 1–9; Sirach 1; 4:11–19; 6:8–31; 14:20–15:10; 24; and Wisdom 6–10. Lady Wisdom existed with God from the beginning and attended creation. She is a pure emanation of the glory of God (Wis. 7:25) and descends from heaven to be with human beings. Wisdom cries out to people (Prov. 1:20–21, 8:1–4; Wis. 6:16), teaches them about things "from above" (see John 3), and, if they will let her, leads them to life. In short, Old Testament Wisdom passages offer many parallels to John's depiction of Jesus.[83] They begin with the invitation to "see."

Jesus's invitation to "come and see" is richly paradigmatic. Throughout the Gospel, Jesus invites people (and the reader) to come along with him and decide where they stand in relation to him, always on the basis of what they experience, "see," what they perceive or understand. Seeing is intrinsically related to John's "signs," miracles, things Jesus does, that people can see and come to believe in him.[84] The great John scholar (of blessed memory) Raymond Brown points out that 1:35–51 and 2:1–11 depict a process whereby "there is a gradual deepening of insight and a profounder realization of who it is that the disciples are following."[85] Characters in the Gospel either reject or respond to Jesus's invitation. If they "come," they increasingly "see." "Following" (discipleship) and understanding are inseparable. Indeed, Jesus (like Wisdom) came into the world to give sight: "I came into this world . . .

so that those who do not see may see" (9:39).
The verse continues, ". . . and those who do see
may become blind." The context of this saying in
chapter 9 is the ironic story of Jesus's giving sight
to a man born blind, and the Pharisees and syna-
gogue leaders who, sighted, are blinded by what
they think they know and who they think could
teach them (9:16, 24, 28–29, 34). Sometimes
"knowing too much," or thinking we do, in fact,
blinds us.

The Johannine Jesus's great "sight promise" is
that "whoever sees me sees him who sent me"
(12:45). When we see Jesus, we see God in a
form that we can appropriate and approach.
This is God, but not the withering God Moses
saw or Job experienced. But I would be remiss
not to note that there is a moral component to
the "seeing," which both the psalmist and John's
Jesus command. This moral component has to do
with how we seek to come before a king (one of
those biblical metaphors for God). Many years
ago, as part of his missionary work in the Middle
East, my late husband visited royalty in the Gulf
states to request funding for his university, which
provided education for their young people. He

was the sort of man who, if pajamas had been sold with neckties, would have bought that kind. Once, wearing slacks, jacket, shirt, and the ubiquitous tie, he met the person who was to take him to the royal audience and was gently sent back to his room to put on a suit because "you are going to see a king."

We too are invited in Psalm 34:8 to "go to see a king." In order to "see" as I have been speaking of it here, we must attend to the moral component implicit in the story of my husband's suit. We must "clean up our act." The holiness codes of the Old Testament are based on the principle that God's holiness requires corresponding holiness in the people God calls and chooses. In Leviticus, God says to Moses, ". . . be holy, for I am holy," and "You shall be holy, for I am holy" (11:44–45). Jesus expresses a similar idea in Matthew's version of the Beatitudes in the Sermon on the Mount. "Blessed are the pure in heart, for *they* shall *see* God" (Matt. 5:8, italics mine; and yes, the root of "see" is *horao*).

Elsewhere in the Psalter, the psalmist helps us understand this Beatitude: "Who shall ascend the hill of the LORD? / And who shall stand in his holy place? / Those who have clean hands and pure hearts" (Ps. 24:3–4a). The term used in the Old Testament for ceremonial purity, "pure" (*katharos* in Greek), does not mean without blemish, but unmixed. The English phrase "one-minded" approaches the meaning. For Jesus, purity did not apply only to sexual behavior (as the term has been used in English since the nineteenth century); it was also an attitude of heart, the center of the person, the most profound level of thought and volition, the center of spiritual life. "Heart" was not the emotive locus, but the organ of reason and will.

This sixth Beatitude (*makarioi*, which, along with the others, should not be translated "happy," but "blessed" in the sense of "you are to be congratulated if . . .") suggests that the only thing that keeps one from "seeing" God comes from within (compare Matt. 15:10–20). Access is not denied from without. The invitation is not just to a moral life but also to one of undivided loyalties. It doesn't mean being sinless (good news!), but speaks to aspiration, to the focus of our deepest desires. The phrase "see God" in this Beatitude implies not only physical perception (it's *horao* after all) but also knowledge of the inner life of God, which is undivided love. To see God we must cultivate purity of heart, the integrated personality that is without mixed motives, that has God as the solitary focus of aspiration and desire. Those who are of one heart (or seek to become so) are more likely in this way to see, to glimpse the reality of God. Perhaps it was his single-minded desire for Jesus that allowed the Beloved Disciple not only to see linen wrappings in an empty tomb but also to believe what they signified (John 20:8).

Not surprisingly, the writer of 1 John brings together the requirement of purity and spiritual sight. He writes, "Beloved, we are God's children now; what we will be has not yet been revealed. What we do know is this: when he is revealed, we will be like him, for we will see him as he is. And all who have this hope in him purify themselves just as he is pure" (1 Jn. 3:2–3). God's children have an extraordinary inheritance connected to the desire to see/know the parent: ". . . we will be like him, for we will see him as he is" is an astonishing promise. And this is not just John's insight. Paul also understood that seeking to see

God is profoundly transformative. He wrote to the Corinthians (that somewhat-less-than-pure church community), "And all of us, with unveiled faces, seeing the glory of the Lord as though reflected in a mirror, are being transformed[86] into the same image from one degree of glory to another" (2 Cor. 3:18). The promise is that we will *become* what we see! C. K. Barrett says of this verse, "Christians seeing in Jesus the image of God, are . . . transformed into the same image; the glory they share with Him ever increasing from one stage of glory to a higher stage."[87]

That we are being remade in the image of what we seek to see is an extraordinary thought. Thus Br. David Steindl-Rast can write, "Beauty seen makes the one who sees it more beautiful. The Presence transforms us into itself. . . ."[88] This is why what we "look at" is so important. It forms and reforms us. For example, I have known for a long time that I can't watch violent films or television programs. Once a violent or gruesome picture imprints itself in my visual memory, it's there, and I never know when it will rerun. What impressionable children see does, indeed, form them. I have enormous anxiety about what violent cartoons and TV programs and video games (the point of which is killing) are doing to young people. If visual beauty in all its manifestations reflects God (as all the major religions suggest), then one who wishes to see God might well seek beauty and avoid ugliness, especially the morally unattractive, revolting, and repulsive. This is why in writing about how Christian communities united in prayer assist the holiness of each member of the community, Lawrence Freeman concludes, "And to see it is to become it."[89] Exactly so.

This focus on the experiential has a long history in Christian teaching. For example, the fourteenth-century Orthodox monk and archbishop Gregory Palamas approached theology not as a conceptual exercise but as an expression of Christian experience. He explored the difference between God's essence and energy, explaining that the transcendent God remains transcendent but communicates the divine self to humanity.[90] Gregory describes with great beauty and simplicity the result of the transformation that occurs as a result of "we will be like him, for we will see him as he is." "Do you not understand that the men . . . who fix their eyes in a divine manner on Him, do not see as we do? . . . the power of the spirit penetrates their human faculties, and allows them to see things which are beyond us." According to Gregory, such persons ". . . know God in God . . . they are united to Him and so have already acquired the form of God."[91] Gregory didn't think the transforming process of seeing was impossible. On the contrary, he knew (he "saw") people in whom it had come to fruition.

Similarly in our own time, in a meditation titled "Seeing God," Lawrence Freeman writes that in "purity of heart we see God. 'Seeing God' is a metaphor. The vision of God cannot be the vision of an object. We cannot know God as an object."[92] But we *can* know, or to use the metaphor of this chapter, see God as the ground of Being, of *our* being (or existence). And when we do so, we recognize in a new way just how close God is (as close, says the Holy Qur'an, as our jugular vein). Sounding a great deal like that lovely old German heretic Meister Eckhart, Freeman says, "The vision of God is seeing God with the vision with which he sees us, the same vision in which he alone sees himself." Freeman continues, "The only precondition for this journey of vision is that we have stopped looking at ourselves and have become still."[93] And that journey, like the journey of Job to turn outward and away from his ego self, as we all know, is a long and arduous one.

"What does it mean to see the Father?" asks Catherine de Hueck Doherty. "It means to assuage that hunger that has been put in man's heart by God himself, the hunger of finally meeting absolute love."[94] And that adds the experience of "taste" to that of "see."

5

EXPERIENCING GOD
Tasting

I have not (recently) been accused, as was Jesus, of being "a glutton and a drunkard" (Matt. 11:19), but I do really enjoy eating and drinking. So if it's about *tasting* that the Lord is good, count me in! "To taste" in Greek implies not only to eat, but also to perceive. In this way "taste" is like "see"; both are metaphors for experience, which includes sense perception and suggests a deeper kind of knowing, a bodily kind. To taste is to partake of something. A well-known Greek lexicon gives as the third synonym of *geuomai*'s first definition, "enjoy."[95] Eating was meant not just for sustaining physical life but also for giving pleasure. Perhaps at least part of our national problem with obesity is not what but how we eat. We eat or ingest without tasting or enjoying, forgetting that a meal feeds more than physical hunger.

In this regard Br. David Steindl-Rast's book on sacred sensuousness reminds us that there is an important connection between seeing and tasting. He speaks of the idiom "a feast for the eyes" as referring "to beauty that feeds our hearts through our eyes."[96] He quotes the Fulani proverb from West Africa that "eyes don't eat, but know what's good to eat," and notes that "Children in India are taught to eat their food first through their eyes, 'like gods,' before putting it into their mouths."[97] I wonder if the good Austrian monk had in mind the distinction between two German words for eating, *fressen*, "to devour," to eat like a beast of prey or like an animal, and *essen*, "to eat, to dine," or to eat like a human being. Enjoying the full, sensuous experience of food is to feed more than the belly. To eat is to ingest. To taste is to savor.

One aspect of the invitation to "taste and see" is the invitation to savor God through God's Word. The psalmist exclaims, "How sweet are your words to my taste, / sweeter than honey to my mouth!" (Ps. 119:103). Jeremiah declares, ". . .

your words were found, and I ate them / and your words became to me a joy and the delight of my heart . . ." (Jer. 15:16). God gives the prophet Ezekiel a scroll (presumably full of words) to eat: ". . . eat this scroll, and go, speak to the house of Israel." The passage continues, ". . . eat this scroll . . . and fill your stomach with it. Then I ate it; and in my mouth it was as sweet as honey" (Ezek. 3:1, 3). The repeated image in the Old Testament of eating God's Word might have been related to a proverb twice quoted by Job, which provides another metaphorical understanding of the senses: "Does not the ear test words / as the palate tastes food?" (Job 12:11; see also 34:3). Apparently some folks literally did "taste and see that the Lord is good." They savored the experience of God through internalizing God's Word.

If, as I suggested in the last chapter, "seeing" is a biblical metaphor for understanding, which in modern parlance we'd call an intellectual function, "taste" can be understood as a metaphor for bodily or *somatic* understanding. We learn not only (and perhaps not primarily) via the intellect, but via the body. Indeed, the body never lies, and learning to listen to it provides access to valuable information. Br. David Steindl-Rast puts the matter elegantly when he says, "The path to God starts at the gates of perception."[98] The command (for it is an imperative) of Psalm 34:8 is that we come to understand or to know God via sensual life as well as via the mind or intellect, and that, I think, is because body knowing is a more holistic (a greatly overused word) or integrated way of knowing.

Let me give two common, if slightly sad, examples. We all have friends or family members who have been stricken by brain injuries or various forms of dementia. They lose cognitive function, but they don't necessarily lose what was learned in the body. When my mother died, my father went into a (blessedly temporary but frightening) sort of grief dementia and couldn't "connect the dots" mentally. But at mother's committal service when I invited those gathered to join in the Twenty-Third Psalm, my father led us in it. It was, like the eaten words and scroll, in his body. Similarly, a dear friend sustained a brain injury as a result of an infection. He couldn't speak or communicate for years. But when a faithful group from his parish came

weekly to sing hymns with him, he sang them
from memory. Those of us who visit what are
euphemistically called "nursing homes" see the
same phenomena. What we know in the body
we *really* know and apparently don't easily lose.

I believe the body is good. God assumed one
in Jesus, the Christ. But Christology is not the
subject of this chapter. It is that the body is one
of God's great gifts to us and is a means of knowing. Human beings are not like the Eldill in C. S.
Lewis's space trilogy. We aren't elongated spirit
beings of light. We were made incarnate, bodily,
somatic. The body is not evil and the mind or
spirit good. Any of the three can be used for
good or evil. St. Paul, who can seem anti-body,
makes a distinction between *soma* ("body," the
whole person) and *sarx* ("flesh," the impermanent
part of *soma*). In itself the body and its wonderful
senses are given for our pleasure. Much of the
poetry of Mary Oliver gloriously makes this
point. For example, human beings don't *have* to
see color to survive. A person can function without perceiving color, but seeing it gives pleasure.
A person can ingest food without tasting it, but
anyone who has lost the sense of taste through

chemotherapy will tell you how diminished the experience is. Taste, too, is gift. You can multiply the examples if you think about it.

It is a pity that in common American parlance "sensuous" and "sexual" are often used synonymously. Sensuous simply means relating to the senses. *Sensual* means "of the flesh," or sensory. I was alarmed to note that my dictionary listed "voluptuous," "worldly," and "irreligious" as synonyms. I am not one of those people who think sex is evil. On the contrary, it is one of God's (very!) good gifts. But confusing sexual experience with sensuous experience can lead to disordered sexuality. Divorce from the senses and from the joy of bodily life can lead to sexual misconduct if the former is confused with the latter. Human bodies are, indeed, designed for reproduction and maintenance of the species (and isn't that fun as well as practical?!). Bodies were also designed to provide us with ways of knowing by receiving all sorts of complex and subtle information.

Matthew Fox has written, "Our senses are meant to serve the heart."[99] "The Heart" is a basic theme in Br. David Steindl-Rast's work.

He writes, "Whenever we speak of the heart, we mean the whole person. Only at heart are we whole. The heart stands for that center of our being where we are one with ourselves, one with all others, one with God."[100] Heart is the center of body. Body-knowing, knowing by means of sight, taste, touch, hearing, smell, and the subtler senses, is for the sake of the heart. According to Br. David, ". . . every sensuous experience is at heart a spiritual one, a divine revelation."[101] He continues, punning deliciously, "Cut off from the senses, dry reasoning turns into non-sense."[102]

Isn't it interesting that the English idiom "coming to one's senses" doesn't mean "senselessness," "craziness," "madness," or indulgence in profligate behavior, but precisely the opposite: returning to rationality, reason, prudence? That which is sense-less is irrational. Without the data of the senses, pure reason (does it exist?) desiccates, or in the extreme, corrupts. Reason and truth are in the body. "O taste *and* see!" In thinking about the senses, it strikes me that it is often, precisely, the need to taste, in its lowest common denominator, hunger, that turns people toward God, that provides what Greek drama calls the *peripatea*, the change in fortune of the hero.

Jesus's parable of the prodigal son once again provides a perfect example. What prompts the parable is the charge that Jesus "welcomes sinners and *eats* with them" (Lk. 15:2, italics mine). In chapter 3 we looked at this parable from the standpoint of the goodness and grace of the father toward unsavory sons. What strikes me in the context of "tasting" God is that it is the younger son's hunger that precipitates his *metanoia* and turns him homeward. We are told, ". . . he began to be in need" (15:14). The need becomes so severe a hunger that this good, Jewish boy is reduced to feeding *pigs* and, worse, wanting to eat their swill. In this degraded condition, "when he came to himself he said, 'How many of my father's hired hands have bread enough and to spare, but here I am dying of hunger'" (15:17). The son's hunger drives him home. The physical reality of his need to eat opens him to the spiritual awakening signaled by the phrase "he came to himself." As a son of his father, when he comes to himself, he returns to his likeness to his father. (Dare I say to the possibility of divinity in himself?) I find his confession genuine and his "pilgrimage" a paradigm of repentance.

The somatic *need* to taste, hunger itself, leads to the prodigal's return. Although the text doesn't explicitly say so, I imagine it was a hunger for more than the food of pigs or of hired hands, but for the father, for reconciliation, for his home, for security, belonging, and love (perhaps even for his grim-faced elder brother). Reflecting on what it means to see the Father, Catherine de Hueck Doherty suggests, "It means to assuage that hunger that has been put in man's heart by God himself, the hunger of finally meeting absolute love. We yearn for it. All of us do."[103] For the prodigal son of the prodigal father, hunger was the origin of the returning, and banqueting was the means of celebrating the return. That thought led me to consider Scripture's many feeding miracles and images of feasting, all of which I take to be invitations to taste and see.

At the outset, God provided for Adam and Eve's hunger: "See, I have given you every plant yielding seed that is upon the face of all the earth, and every tree with seed in its fruit; you shall have them for food" (Gen. 1:29). In Old Testament feeding miracles, God provides something *to* taste. A most dramatic example is the miraculous feeding in the wilderness after the exodus from Egypt. All of Exodus 16 is devoted to God's response to the Israelites' hunger, their longing for the bread and fleshpots of Egypt (Exod. 16:3). God provides manna, which "was like coriander seed, white, and the taste of it was like wafers made with honey" (Exod. 16:31). "The people went around and gathered it, ground it in mills or beat it in pots and made cakes of it; and the taste of it was like the taste of cakes baked with oil" (Num. 11:8). Interestingly, God's plan was "daily bread" collected according to individual need. Each person was to take what was needed for the day. If manna were hoarded, it "bred worms and became foul" (Exod. 16:20). The people were being taught to trust God day by day to supply their hungers. God provided this palatable food for forty years, until they reached the border of Canaan.[104]

The prophet Elijah the Tishbite (nemesis of Queen Jezebel) was also miraculously fed. When at God's direction Elijah lived by the Wadi Cherith, "The ravens brought him bread and meat in the morning, and bread and meat in the evening; and he drank from the wadi" (1 Kgs. 17:6). Thereafter, again by divine direction, he went to Zarephath and asked a widow for a drink of water, only to discover she was gathering sticks to cook a last meal for herself and her son ". . . that we may eat it, and die" (1 Kgs. 17:12). In response to her sharing "a little cake," Elijah promises on God's behalf that "The jar of meal will not be emptied and the jug of oil will not fail" until the drought is over. "The jar of meal *was not* emptied, neither did the jug of oil fail, according to the word of the LORD that he spoke by Elijah" (1 Kgs. 17:14, 16, italics mine). After beating the priests of Baal at their own game (and then slaughtering them, 1 Kgs. 18:20–40), Elijah flees from Jezebel to the wilderness where an angel delivers his meals (1 Kgs. 18:5–7). As in Israel's wilderness sojourn, miraculous food is given so that God's servant can "taste" God's goodness in provision for the body.

I suspect that when we think of biblical feeding stories, we think first of Jesus's feeding the multitudes. For the Evangelist Mark, Jesus the provider of food is an example of the *chrestos* of the Christ at least twice before the Last Supper. In chapter 6 Jesus attempts to take the apostles on a little vacation, but a crowd gathers ". . . and he had compassion for them because they were like sheep without a shepherd, and he began to teach them . . ." (6:34). When the teaching is finished, Jesus recognizes the bodily need of the crowd for food, but they are in "a deserted place." The root word for "desert" appears three times (6:30, 32, 35) so that the reader doesn't miss the allusion to God's earlier feeding during the wilderness sojourn of the Exodus. The disciples are charged to feed the crowd but find the task impossible. Taking what is available, five loaves and two fish, Jesus "looked up to heaven, and blessed and broke the loaves and gave them to his disciples to set before the people" (6:41). Mark's use of what we recognize as Eucharistic language is certainly deliberate. Like the Israelites in the Sinai, the people "all ate and were filled" (6:42), but unlike them, twelve baskets of leftovers are collected.

In Mark 8, there is a second feeding miracle. Some scholars think it is a "doublet," a retelling of the original miracle. I think it's another feeding altogether. The first was in Jewish territory.

The second is in "the region of the Decapolis" (7:31). In 7:24–30 in Tyre (a Gentile city), a *Syrophoenician* (wrong nationality, wrong religion) woman has reminded Jesus of the hunger of Gentiles. In 8:1–10 Jesus has "compassion for the crowd, because they have been with me now for three days and have nothing to eat" (8:2). So there is a second feeding, again using Eucharistic language (8:6), this time in *Gentile* territory and again with leftovers. Jesus responds to the hunger of Jew and Gentile alike. To each community he inclusively says by his actions, "taste and see."[105]

Mark must have known that Jewish expectations of the Messiah included an Eschatological Banquet. In the last days when the Messiah came, he was to host a great banquet to which all would be invited, and *only* the Messiah could provide this banquet. Indeed, Luke's Jesus declares, "Then people will come from the east and west, from north and south, and will eat in the kingdom of God" (Lk. 13:29). Most New Testament images of heaven include banquets and feasting. (Set a place for me!) In fact, in Luke's beloved story of the Emmaus Road (to which we shall return in the conclusion), the risen Jesus, the Christ, is recognized when he serves as host at table. "When he was at the table with them, he took bread, blessed and broke it, and gave it to them. Then their eyes were opened, and they recognized him . . . " (Lk. 24:30–31).

By the time Mark, Matthew, and Luke were written (probably between AD 65 and 85), the Lord's Supper, the earliest account of which occurs in Paul's first letter to the Corinthians (ca. AD 55) had circulated for twenty years. Already by the 50s the practice was so important that the "words of institution" (1 Cor. 11:23–26) constituted the central bit of a teaching in which Paul seeks to correct abuses in its practice (1 Cor. 11:17–26). One of the most immediate and tangible ways Jesus fulfilled the promise to remain with the disciples after he went away ("I will not leave you orphaned; I am coming to you," John 14:18) was understood by the ancient church to be the Lord's Supper. What Jesus did, and in particular what Jesus *gave* "on the night before he was betrayed" (1 Cor. 11:23; Mark 14:22–25), became a tasteable way he remained with them—and with us. He offered his body (himself) and his blood (his life) to feed his friends. In the Eucharist, we take the very self and life of Jesus into our selves, our bodies and lives, as spiritual food, heavenly food, manna. And like manna, the eating must be regular and renewed. Remember, Psalm 34 has traditionally been used by the Orthodox Church at the time of Communion. In the words of the Orthodox Study Bible, "Verse 8 is seen throughout the Orthodox Church as describing the act of receiving the Body and Blood of Christ. . . . Verse 8 was the communion hymn on all Sundays of the year for many centuries."[106]

Far too large a percentage of the world's population is chronically undernourished, and these hungers are both bodily and spiritual. If there are hungers, God is prepared to assuage them. When it comes to physical hunger, I think God's plan must be like that of Jesus in the Mark 6 feeding story. He says to the disciples, *"You give them something to eat"* (Mk. 6:37, italics mine). The loaves and fishes we have, whether they are financial or organizational or whatever, are to be used for those upon whom Jesus has compassion. When it comes to spiritual hunger, God has taken the matter into his own hands, blessed, broken, and given the only beloved Son for and to us.

The dialogue that makes up seventeenth-century English priest and poet George Herbert's poem "Love (III)" could be that of Jesus with any one of us. "Love bade me welcome: yet my soul drew back / Guiltie of dust and sinne." Love (the personification of Jesus in the poem) continually invites the speaker, who repeats his own unworthiness. The poem closes, "you must sit down, says Love, and taste my meat: / So I did sit and eat."[107]

"O taste and see how good the Lord is."

CONCLUSION

"Taste and see that the LORD is good" is an invitation—indeed, a command—to experience God, not in some rarefied, sacred environment, but as potentially discernible in everything, everywhere. Writing about the great Jesuit theologian Karl Rahner, Robert Ellsberg reminds us that Rahner "believed that all human existence is rooted in the holy and infinite mystery of God. Religious experience is thus not a separate category of existence; it is the potential for a certain quality or depth available in our everyday life. Human nature is created with an openness to God."[108] Indeed, the simple act of breathing, the life of the senses, seeing and tasting, such common, almost banal activities, provide entrée to the divine. God isn't somewhere else, but exactly where we are in this present moment. The invitation to "taste and see" reminds us of that. Being fully awake in the aliveness of incarnate life is drawing near to God.

The God Who Is and Who is manifested in goodness, graciousness, and generosity has given us life and, therefore, bodies with which to explore and experience the Divine Self. The life of the mind and of the senses is rich, but either alone is inadequate to this huge and happy task. Together they provide extraordinary understanding—after they are taken to and transformed by the heart. As Lawrence Freeman has written, ". . . when the heart sees . . . there is perfect response. A knowledge is born which is not that of the outsider or the observer but is of one who participates in what is known. The Knowing One is God who calls us to know him, to see him and to love him by being totally one with him."[109] As I indicated in chapter 4, we are changed in this process, changed into Whom we see and taste. Our metamorphosis will probably not be "in a moment, in the twinkling of an eye" (1 Cor. 15:52), but, over a lifetime, we *will* be changed into the likeness of what we give our hearts to. As Br. David Steindl-Rast so beautifully puts it, "we become that to which we give ourselves with all our senses."[110]

One of the most loved resurrection appearances of Jesus in the Gospels is Luke's account of the encounter on the road to Emmaus. This episode provides a dramatic example of the "marriage" of seeing and tasting, which links us to those same powerful experiences in Christian liturgy. On the first day of the week, two disciples of Jesus are walking *away* from Jerusalem. (That itself is a poignant image.) They have heard that Jesus has been raised, but are examples of those to whom the women's ". . . words seemed . . . an idle tale, and they did not believe them" (Lk. 24:11). They are joined by Jesus, ". . . but their eyes were kept from recognizing him" (24:16). They see (*blepo*) but are kept from seeing (*horao*), perhaps in order to receive further instruction. As they walk along, the two recount the recent events in Jerusalem. Jesus interprets the meaning of those events: ". . . beginning with Moses and all the prophets, he interpreted to them the things about himself in all the scriptures" (24:27). To see is to understand, and understanding comes by means of the word (Scripture) and the Word (Jesus). This is what we, too, can receive in the first half of the liturgy, the liturgy of the word.

When the trio arrives at Emmaus, the two disciples urge the still-unrecognized Jesus to stay with them. They share a meal, at which Jesus ". . . took bread, blessed and broke it, and gave it to them" (24:30). Luke carefully reproduces the Eucharistic words of institution, and continues, "Then their eyes were opened, and they recognized him; and he vanished from their sight" (24:31). Perhaps they were kept from recognizing Jesus because word alone was not enough to facilitate complete sight. In order to see, the two travelers had to taste, to take Jesus into themselves as he (again) offered them the bread that was his body. This we too receive in the second half of the liturgy, the liturgy of the Table, of Sacrament.

The postresurrection encounter with Jesus on the way and at Emmaus suggests that tasting and seeing go together. They represent the bodily knowledge of the senses (taste) and the intellectual knowledge (sight) brought together and perfected in the presence of Jesus. Here is how Dom Andre Louf describes it: "Those who are called to recognize the risen Jesus do so by following the . . . two-pronged path: by the sacrament of Jesus' body and that of his Word, touching Jesus' body and understanding the Scriptures. These two . . . in a mysterious way, contain the Risen One and . . . in every Eucharist make him present to all who believe."[111]

Every traditional Christian liturgy offers the invitation and the opportunity to taste and see, to share the experience of the Emmaus disciples, whose hearts were ". . . burning within . . . while he was talking . . . on the road, while he was opening the scriptures" (24:32) and to whom "he had been made known . . . in the breaking of the bread" (24:35). The experience of God's reality is certainly available everywhere. But it is especially accessible in Christian liturgy, which *embodies* the invitation to "taste and see."

The Emmaus account is a pilgrimage story; it happened "on the road" (24:35). The disciples are on the way, not at the destination. The invitation to taste and see that God is good is not a "one off," but an invitation to an ongoing journey, as well as to what we are called to experience over and over again as we travel. The great paradigm is, of course, the Exodus-Sinai event in which the Hebrews are summoned to liberation, invited while they are dressed for travel to eat a meal, and then fed (for forty years) by God in the wilderness of the journey itself. *In* the wilderness, *on* the way, word (the "ten words," the Decalogue), and heavenly food (manna) are provided, day by day. They had to trust God *daily* for provision (water, food, direction), for manifestation of divine graciousness. They had to give themselves to the journey.

We, too, are called to give ourselves to this journey and to the root story, which is "how good the Lord is," the reality of God as good and gracious, manifested in what God allows us to taste and to see. This isn't easy because it involves self-giving to a plot that we don't create, to accept a role prepared for us in a great drama *that we don't write*. It is, in short, to surrender to God. Surrender is costly, but in the particular story to which we are invited, it is, paradoxically, our victory. It is to say with the heroes of the Old Testament, "Here I am," to cry out with the father of the spirit possessed son, "I believe; help my unbelief" (Mk. 9:24), to whisper with Mary of Nazareth, ". . . let it be with me according to your word" (Lk. 1:38).

What other word is there? In *Gratefulness, The Heart of Prayer* Br. David Steindl-Rast says of "word" that it "is the basic biblical truth that

'God speaks.' If God speaks, the whole universe and everything in it is word. This is the biblical way of saying that everything makes sense the moment we listen with the heart. We will find this to be true if we have the courage to listen. That courage is called faith."[112] It is this courage and faith that Peter exhibits when, after some disciples leave Jesus because his "teaching is difficult; who can accept it?" (John 6:60), and Jesus asks the Twelve if they want to go too, he responds, "Lord, to whom can we go? You have the words of eternal life" (John 6:68).

They aren't hidden words. They are the manna God wants to offer, the door God wants to open, the life of freedom and joy and aliveness that God wants to give. But you can't stand by the side of the lake. You have to plunge in. You can't stand by the road and watch the parade go by. This journey is not a spectator sport. You have to trudge on up the road, to play in the game. You get an invitation, but it is not to think abstractly about God, but to experience God (taste and see). You have to respond, to look and see, to risk tasting the fare in order to experience the Reality (how good the Lord is). "O taste and see that the LORD is good" is a half verse. The second half is the promise that completes the challenge, "Happy are those who take refuge in him" (Ps. 34:8).

ACKNOWLEDGMENTS

It was an enormous surprise and great honor to be asked by Paraclete Press to write an extended meditation on Psalm 34:8. I am immensely grateful for that opportunity and for the kind solicitude of editor Jon Sweeney, who was consistently, gently encouraging and provided the best sort of editorial comments on the initial drafts. Thanks to Robert Edmonson and the Paraclete Press staff for bringing the draft to printed copy and to Sr. Madeleine Cleverly who is making the book known. Each was patient with my archaic way of working. I am grateful to Sr. Mary Ann Rosenbaum, CSJ, for her skill as a photographer and her generosity in providing my "portrait."

Readers will notice how frequently Br. David Steindl-Rast, OSB, is quoted in this book. I met Br. David thirty-five years ago at St. Paul's Memorial Episcopal Church (mentioned in the introduction and a community for which I shall always be grateful and to whom again I say, "thank you").

He has played a crucial role in my spiritual development ever since. I am delighted to express my gratitude. If this book has done nothing else positive, it has introduced you to Br. David.

Much of the methodology of biblical theology upon which this meditation rests I learned from my revered colleague and friend at Pittsburgh Theological Seminary, Dr. Donald E. Gowan, to whom my indebtedness is profound. Our team-taught course on biblical theology was my favorite assignment, but any misuse of method or erroneous conclusions are my own.

Finally, I thank my teachers and their teachers, my students and their students. May we form an unbroken procession giving "light to those who sit in darkness and in the shadow of death" until "the Dawn from on high has broken upon us" (Luke 1:78–79).

The Anchorage, Wheeling, WV
July 31, 2013
Feast of St. Ignatius of Loyola

NOTES

Introduction

1   You can find a beautiful rendition of this music (and a good review of the history of English church music) on The Cambridge Singers CD *Faire is the Heaven*, Collegium Records (1988).

1 THE PHRASE:
Text and Context

2   Margaret M. Daly-Denton, *Psalm-Shaped Prayerfulness: A Guide to the Christian Reception of the Psalms* (Collegeville, MN: Liturgical Press, 2011), 63.

3   Kathleen Norris, preface to *The Psalms* (New York: Riverhead, 1997), viii.

4   Ibid., ix.

5   Thomas Merton, *Praying the Psalms* (Collegeville, MN: Liturgical Press, 1956), 16, 31.

6   Quoted in Kathleen Norris, *The Cloister Walk* (New York: Riverhead, 1996), 91.

7   William L. Holladay, *The Psalms through Three Thousand Years: Prayerbook of a Cloud of Witnesses* (Minneapolis: Fortress, 1993).

8   Merton, *Praying the Psalms*, 11.

9   Roland E. Murphy, "The Psalms: Prayer of Israel and the Church," *The Bible Today* 32, no. 3 (1994): 136.

10   Recent scholarship is exploring "collections within the collection" and interpretations of individual psalms in relation to where they appear in the whole Psalter. See Margaret M. Daly-Denton, *Psalm-Shaped Prayerfulness*, which provides an accessible introduction to this approach. See note 2 above.

11   Mitchell Dahood, *Psalms I*, Anchor Bible Commentary (Garden City, NY: Doubleday, 1965), 205.

12   Roland E. Murphy, *The Gift of the Psalms* (Peabody, MA: Hendrickson, 2000), 87.

13   Murphy, *Gift of the Psalms*, 11.

14   Walter J. Harrelson, gen. ed., *The New Interpreter's Study Bible* (Nashville: Abingdon, 2003), 780.

15   See, for example, S. E. Gillingham, *The Poems and Psalms of the Hebrew Bible* (New York: Oxford University Press, 1994), 228. We shall return to Wisdom Literature, and the figure of Lady Wisdom, later.

16 *The Psalms* (popularly known as "The Grail Edition" for singing) (Mahwah, NJ: Paulist Press, 1966), 66.

17 Note on 3:8 in *The New Interpreter's Study Bible*, 780.

18 Eugene H. Peterson, *The Message*, New Testament with Psalms and Proverbs (Colorado Springs, CO: NavPress, 1993), 400.

19 Dahood, *Psalms I*, 204.

20 Ibid., 206.

21 J. H. Moulton and G. Milligan, *The Vocabulary of the Greek New Testament* (Grand Rapids, MI: Eerdmans, 1930/1980), 455.

22 W. F. Arndt and F. W. Gingrich, *A Greek-English Lexicon of the New Testament and Other Early Christian Literature* (Chicago: University of Chicago Press, 1952/1957), 581.

23 Murphy, *Gift of the Psalms*, 25, and see the work of Daly-Denton, note 2, above.

24 Holladay, *Psalms*, 169.

25 Ibid., 180. The italics in the text are Holladay's.

26 *The Orthodox Study Bible*, ed. Joseph Allen et al. (Nashville: Thomas Nelson, 1993), 661.

27 Holladay, *Psalms*, 184.

28 See, for example, *Pilgrim Hymnal* (Boston: Pilgrim, 1931/1961), no. 81.

29 Helpful suggestions for praying the Psalter can be found in John C. Endres and Elizabeth

Liebert, *A Retreat with the Psalms: Resources for Personal and Communal Prayer* (Mahwah, NJ: Paulist Press, 2001), and in chap. 2 of my book *For God Alone: A Primer on Prayer* (Notre Dame: University of Notre Dame Press, 2009).

2 THE LORD *IS*

30 For an interesting meditation on this point, see Stephen Sullivan, "Foolishness!" *America Magazine*, February 11, 2013, 11–14, and Bonnie Thurston, *Maverick Mark: Untaming the First Gospel* (Collegeville, MN: Liturgical Press, 2013).

31 Br. David Steindl-Rast, *Deeper than Words: Living the Apostles' Creed* (New York: Image/Doubleday, 2010), 24.

32 Alister McGrath, *"I Believe": Exploring the Apostles' Creed* (Downers Grove, IL: InterVarsity Press, 1991/1997), 20.

33 Ibid., 21.

34 Steindl-Rast, *Deeper than Words*, 24.

35 Ibid.

36 Br. David Steindl-Rast, *Gratefulness, The Heart of Prayer* (New York: Palest Press, 1984), 198.

37 Catherine de Hueck Doherty from *Re-Entry Into Faith*, quoted in *Magnificat*, March 2013, 210.

38   *The Poems of Gerard Manley Hopkins*, 4th ed., ed. W. H. Gardner and H. H. MacKenzie (New York: Oxford University Press, 1970), 66.

39   Quoted in Dana Greene, *Denise Levertov: A Poet's Life* (Chicago: University of Illinois Press, 2012), 173.

40   Denise Levertov, *Sands of the Well* (New York: New Directions, 1996), 129.

41   Dorothee Soelle, *Theology for Skeptics: Reflections on God* (Minneapolis: Fortress Press, 1995), 112.

42   W. T. Davison, "GOD (Biblical and Christian)," in *Encyclopedia of Religion and Ethics*, ed. James Hastings (New York: Charles Scribner's Sons, 1914), 6:253–54.

43   Ibid., 6:254.

44   Jack Miles, *God: A Biography* (New York: Alfred A. Knopf, 1995), 6.

45   John F. Kavanaugh, "Holy Ground of Being," *America*, March 11, 1995, 39.

46   S. David Sperling, "God in the Hebrew Scriptures," in *The Encyclopedia of Religion*, ed. Mircea Eliade (New York: Macmillan, 1987), 6:1.

47   Donald E. Gowan, *Theology in Exodus* (Louisville: Westminster John Knox Press, 1994), 85.

48   Ibid., 86.

49   Ibid., 87.

50   Ibid., 96.

51   Mary Daly, *Beyond God the Father* (Boston: Beacon Press, 1973), 33–34.

52   Ibid., 34.

53   Soelle, *Theology for Skeptics*, 49.

54   Ibid., 16.

55   G.W.H. Lampe, *God as Spirit* (Oxford: Oxford University Press, 1977), 176–77.

56   Hugh of St. Victor, *De Arca Noe morali* 1.2, quoted in Davison, "GOD," 264.

3 THE LORD IS *GOOD*

57   A very good biblical introduction to the matter is found in part 3, "The Attributes of God" in the entry "God" by D. Guthrie and R. P. Martin in *Dictionary of Paul and His Letters*, ed. G. F. Hawthorne, R. P. Martin, and D. G. Reid (Downers Grove, IL: InterVarsity Press, 1993), 354–69.

58   R.T.A. Murphy, "Nature of God in Biblical Theology," in *New Catholic Encyclopedia* (New York: McGraw-Hill, 1967), 6:560.

59   K. Weiss, "*Chrestos*," in *Theological Dictionary of the New Testament* (abridged in one volume), ed. Geoffrey W. Bromiley (Grand Rapids: Eerdmans, 1985/1992), 1320.

60   A beautiful and moving consideration of Psalm 119 is Margaret B. Ingraham's *The Holy Alphabet: Lyric Poems Adapted from Psalm 119* (Brewster, MA: Paraclete Press, 2009).

61   Weiss, "*Chrestos*," 1321.

62   Ibid., 1322.

63   Guthrie and Martin, "God," 364.

64   J. I. Packer, *Knowing God* (Downers Grove, IL: InterVarsity Press, 1973), 117.

65   Ibid., 119.

66   Ibid., 120.

67   Ibid.

68   Gerald O'Collins, SJ, and Edward G. Farrugia, SJ, *A Concise Dictionary of Theology* (New York: Paulist Press, 1991), 21.

69   In the sonnet "Spring," in *Poems of Gerard Manley Hopkins*, 67 (see note 38 above).

70   Lawrence S. Cunningham, *Things Seen and Unseen: A Catholic Theologian's Notebook* (Notre Dame, IN: Sorin, 2010), 208.

4 EXPERIENCING GOD
Seeing

71   I read the full text in Lyn Klug, ed., *Soul Weavings: A Gathering of Women's Prayers* (Minneapolis: Augsburg, 1996), 88.

72   Karl Barth, *Credo*, trans. J. Strathearn McNab (New York: Charles Scribner's Sons, 1936), 12–13.

73   W. Michaelis, "horáō, et al," in *Theological Dictionary of the New Testament*, 706 (see note 59, above).

74   Ibid., 709.

75   Jacques Maritain, *Approaches to God* (New York: Macmillan, 1954/1967), xi. Maritain uses the masculine pronoun here.

76   Ibid., 97.

77   *Chandogya Upanishad* 6.8.6. Quoted in Maritain, *Approaches to God*, 103.

78   Robert F. Morneau, "Juice and Joy," *Give Us This Day*, April 2013, 6.

79   It's worth remembering that the books of Maccabees suggest that God's people can suffer *because* they are righteous. See especially 2 Macc. 6:12–17.

80   *The New Oxford Annotated Bible with the Apocrypha*, expanded ed., RSV (New York: Oxford University Press, 1977), 654–55.

81 Although my reading differs from each of theirs, I am grateful for the immense amount I have learned about Job from the lectures of professors Donald E. Gowan and Kathleen M. O'Connor.

82 Perhaps ironically, at the close of the Gospel, the Johannine Jesus suggests faith need not rest on direct experience of his incarnate self. "Have you believed because you have seen me? Blessed are those who have not seen and yet have come to believe" (20:29). Jesus suggests there are various *ways* of "seeing."

83 Raymond E. Brown, *The Gospel According to John* (i–xii) Anchor Bible (New York: Doubleday, 1966), 79, and see CXXII–CXXV. For more, see Raymond E. Brown, *An Introduction to the Gospel of John*, ed. Francis J. Moloney (New York: Doubleday, 2003), especially "Wisdom Motifs," 259–65.

84 The seven signs include (1) the miracle at Cana (chap. 2); (2) the healing of an official's child (chap. 4); (3) a healing in Jerusalem (chap. 5); (4) a feeding (chap. 6); (5) walking on the water (chap. 6); (6) healing a blind man (chap. 9); (7) and raising Lazarus (chap. 11), which is the prototype of God's great sign: the resurrection of Jesus.

References to signs in the Gospel include 2:23; 4:45; 7:4; 7:37; and see 20:30.

85   Brown, *Gospel*, 77.

86   The verb *metamorphoomai* ("to change or inwardly transform") is a perfect passive participle. The passive means that something is being done *to* us; we are acted upon, not initiators of the action. The perfect indicates ongoing action resulting from something previously done.

87   C. K. Barrett, *The Second Epistle to the Corinthians* (London: Adam and Charles Black, 1973), quoted in Fritz Rienecker and Cleon Rogers, *Linguistic Key to the Greek New Testament* (Grand Rapids: Zondervan, 1976), 461–62. The original has "w." for the "with," which I have supplied for clarity's sake.

88   Br. David Steind-Rast, *A Listening Heart: The Spirituality of Sacred Sensuousness* (New York: Crossroad, 1983/1999), 42.

89   Lawrence Freeman, *Light Within* (New York: Crossroad, 1987), 46.

90   *Gregory Palamas: The Triads*, ed. John Meyendorff, Classics of Western Spirituality (New York: Paulist Press, 1983), 6 and 20.

91   Ibid, 107, 109.

92   Freeman, *Light Within*, 79.

93   Ibid., 79–80.

94   Catherine de Hueck Doherty, *Re-Entry Into Faith* (2012) quoted in *Magnificat*, March 2013, 211.

5 EXPERIENCING GOD
Tasting

95 Arndt and Gingrich, *A Greek-English Lexicon*, 156 (see note 22, above). "Enjoy" is the translation when used with the accusative.

96 Steindl-Rast, *Listening Heart*, 58 (see note 88, above).

97 Ibid.

98 Ibid., 27.

99 Quoted in ibid., xiii.

100 Steindl-Rast, *Gratefulness*, 202.

101 Steindl-Rast, *Listening Heart*, 18.

102 Ibid., 19.

103 Catherine de Hueck Doherty, quoted in *Magnificat*, March 2013, 211.

104 Forty years is a long time to eat the same thing however delicious it is. For a story about that problem, see Numbers 11.

105 Jesus's inclusivity in the feedings would have been of particular interest to Mark who was probably writing to a mixed community of Gentile and Jewish Christians in Rome. Mark's Gospel evinces a particular interest in the Gentile mission, as, of course, does St. Paul's Letter to the Romans.

106 Note in *The Orthodox Study Bible*, 661 (see note 26, above).

107 *The Works of George Herbert*, ed. F. E. Hutchinson (Oxford: Clarendon Press, 1941/1972), 188–89.

Conclusion

108 Robert Ellsberg, "Karl Rahner," *Give Us This Day*, March 2013, 302.

109 Freeman, *Light Within*, 103 (see note 89, above).

110 Steindl-Rast, *A Listening Heart*, 42 (see note 88, above).

111 Dom Andre Louf, *Mercy in Weakness*, quoted in *Magnificat*, April 2013, 77.

112 Steindl-Rast, *Gratefulness*, 222 (see note 36, above).

ABOUT PARACLETE PRESS

Who We Are

Paraclete Press is a publisher of books, recordings, and DVDs on Christian spirituality. Our publishing represents a full expression of Christian belief and practice—from Catholic to Evangelical; from Protestant to Orthodox.

We are the publishing arm of the Community of Jesus, an ecumenical monastic community in the Benedictine tradition. As such, we are uniquely positioned in the marketplace without connection to a large corporation and with informal relationships to many branches and denominations of faith.

What We Are Doing

Books | Paraclete publishes books that show the richness and depth of what it means to be Christian. Although Benedictine spirituality is at the heart of all that we do, we publish books that reflect the Christian experience across many cultures, time periods, and houses of worship. We publish books that nourish the vibrant life of the church and its people—books about spiritual practice, formation, history, ideas, and customs.

We have several different series, including the best-selling Paraclete Essentials and Paraclete Giants series of classic texts in contemporary English; Voices from the Monastery—men and women monastics writing about living a spiritual life today; award-winning poetry; best-selling gift books for children on the occasions of baptism and first communion; and the Active Prayer Series that brings creativity and liveliness to any life of prayer.

Recordings | From Gregorian chant to contemporary American choral works, our music recordings celebrate sacred choral music through the centuries. Paraclete distributes the recordings of the internationally acclaimed choir Gloriæ Dei Cantores, praised for their "rapt and fathomless spiritual intensity" by *American Record Guide*, and the Gloriæ Dei Cantores Schola, which specializes in the study and performance of Gregorian chant. Paraclete is also the exclusive North American distributor of the recordings of the Monastic Choir of St. Peter's Abbey in Solesmes, France, long considered to be a leading authority on Gregorian chant.

Videos | Our videos offer spiritual help, healing, and biblical guidance for life issues: grief and loss, marriage, forgiveness, anger management, facing death, and spiritual formation.

Learn more about us at our website: www.paracletepress.com, or call us toll-free at 1-800-451-5006.

SCAN
TO
READ
MORE

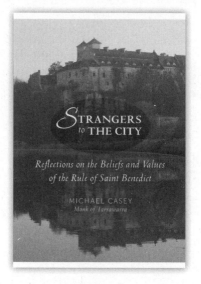

STRANGERS TO THE CITY
Michael Casey

ISBN: 978-1-61261-397-0 | $15.99, Paperback

Eloquent and incisive, Casey invites you to embrace the challenge of gospel living, which is opposed to the dominant, secular culture.

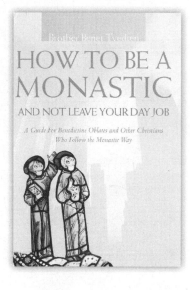

How to Be a Monastic and Not Leave Your Day Job
Br. Benet Tvedten

ISBN: 978-1-61261-414-4 | $14.99, Paperback

This essential guide explains how people who live and work in "the world" are still invited to balance work with prayer, cultivate interdependence with others, practice hospitality, and otherwise practice their spirituality like monks.

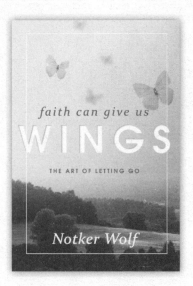